GHOSTIES AND GHOULIES AND LONG-LEGGED BEASTIES AND THINGS THAT GO BUMP IN THE NIGHT

GHOSTIES AND GHOULIES AND LONG-LEGGED BEASTIES AND THINGS THAT GO BUMP IN THE NIGHT

Christian Basics for the Twenty-First Century

Don E. Post, Ph.D.

iUniverse, Inc.
New York   Lincoln   Shanghai

GHOSTIES AND GHOULIES AND LONG-LEGGED BEASTIES
AND THINGS THAT GO BUMP IN THE NIGHT
Christian Basics for the Twenty-First Century

Copyright © 2004 by Donald E. Post

All rights reserved. No part of this book may be used or reproduced by any means, graphic, electronic, or mechanical, including photocopying, recording, taping or by any information storage retrieval system without the written permission of the publisher except in the case of brief quotations embodied in critical articles and reviews.

iUniverse books may be ordered through booksellers or by contacting:

iUniverse
2021 Pine Lake Road, Suite 100
Lincoln, NE 68512
www.iuniverse.com
1-800-Authors (1-800-288-4677)

ISBN: 0-595-33489-X (Pbk)
ISBN: 0-595-66954-9 (Cloth)

Printed in the United States of America

To My Grandchildren: Ben and Grace Carlson

CONTENTS

About the Title—Page ix

Preface—Page xi

First Letter—Page 1
Ghosties & Ghoulies & Long-Legged-Beasties & Things
That Go Bump In The Night

Second Letter—Page 16
the Bible: Magic, Mysticism Or Faith

Third Letter—Page 26
The Early Hebrews & Christians

Fourth Letter—Page 47
Shaa-zam & Presto! The Christian Bible

Fifth Letter—Page 59
Beauty and the Beast

Sixth Letter—Page 73
The Mystery Man

Seventh Letter—Page 86
The Whisper From a Burning Bush

Eighth Letter—Page 97
The End of Religion

Ninth Letter—Page 105
From Barbarism To Renaissance
500 C.E.–1500 C.E.

Don E. Post, Ph.D.

Tenth Letter—Page 127
The Oppressed Become The Oppressors
1500–1900 C.E.

Eleventh Letter—Page 141
Dawn Of The Modern Age
18th Century

Twelfth Letter—Page 158
The Fractured Church
1900–Present

Thirteenth Letter—Page 177
The Epilogue

ABOUT THE TITLE

An Early Cornish Litany

Laity: O Lord, deliver us from Ghosties and Ghoulies and long-legged beasties and things that go bump in the night.

Clergy: O' Lord, deliver us.

Lest one thinks I am trying to be funny, this phrase was reportedly part of a 14th or 15th Century Protestant litany, probably Cornish, although sources within the Anglican Church have not been able to locate the total litany. This may seem humorous now, but it represents a world filled with scary creatures. Unfortunately, that eerie world still exists for too many. This superstitious world view hang-over is a good example of what social scientists call *cultural lag*.

PREFACE

A number of events of the last few decades have contributed to my desire to set forth a basic road map of the Christian faith for my grandchildren as I've come to understand it. First, I'm concerned about the rise of *all* religious fundamentalisms throughout the world (Christian, Moslem, Jewish). Not being a Muslin or a Jew I cannot address their dilemma except to note that all fundamentalists share a common *fear of modernity.*

Second, in 1993, after several decades away from the active pastoral ministry, I accepted a small country church out of Huntsville, Texas, and served it for eight years. To my surprise the laity were hungry for something other than worn-out clichés and hand-me-down beliefs. They weren't afraid to look at Scripture as a human product of a particular age, albeit inspired. Most were not willing to sacrifice their intelligence on the altar of a mindless literalistic biblical worldview.

Third, I am stunned by the tumultuous to do created by Mel Gibson's movie, *The Passion of the Christ* and fueled by novels such as *The DiVinci Code*, which is supposed to be out in movie form soon. Since Gibson's movie reportedly earned $250 million in three weeks, movie moguls are cooking up further fare for the Christians. These mass media portrayals of Biblical events have forced to the surface a great deal of Biblical illiteracy among Christians.

In the following *letters* to my grandchildren, *Ben* and *Grace Carlson*, I've tried to peel away the extraneous ideological debris that circulates in Christendom in order to more clearly reveal this historic God-man **Mystery** for people daring to live an honest intellectual life in the 21st Century. A Christological thread seeks to tie the letters together. Minimally I hope my thoughts and observations will provide Ben and Grace a safe launching pad for their life's trek because I doubt I will be ticking when they are old enough to wrestle with these complex issues. But I also hope that those reading over their shoulders will find some of their taken-for-granted Christian views challenged. We all need to pull up our theological ideas by the roots from time to time and rethink them. Much of our contemporary Christian beliefs are hand-me-downs from medieval lore and superstition.

Don E. Post, Ph.D.

Last, writing in a *letters* style allows me to use colloquial language and express my own sentiments. Please note that I refer to the time before and after the Jesus event as B.C.E. (before the common era) and C.E. (common era).

As I write these letters I often felt that Saint Simon was looking over my shoulder and warning me to avoid his writing faults. He once wrote:

> Shall I add a word about the style—its carelessness, the same words recurring too close together, too many synonyms, especially the long sentences that cause obscurity, and perhaps repetitions of facts. I am aware of these faults. I couldn't avoid them, carried away by the matter and inattentive to the manner of conveying it, not to say explaining it. I haven't been able to cure myself of writing too fast.
> —Saint Simon, *Memoirs*.

Being forewarned I painstakingly tried to avoid these errors.

FIRST LETTER

Ghosties & Ghoulies & Long-Legged-Beasties & Things That Go Bump In The Night

Dear Ben and Grace,

It will be a number of years before either of you will understand the content of these letters. But the time will come when you will seriously ponder the meaning of the universe and have the skill to understand what I've written. You will struggle with the biblical records and the nature of the Christian faith. I would love to be present when you reach this stage because you will be overwhelmed by many voices, all claiming to be ultimate truth and demanding your undying allegiance. Since I may not be there when you enter that phase of your life the following reflections are my attempt to share with you what I've learned during my own pilgrimage. They are offered in hopes you both will avoid some of the pitfalls suffered by others.

Biblical and religious naiveté is fairly widespread and I don't want either of you to suffer the same fate. As a simple example of this problem, your Uncle Darren recently sent me some 5th and 6th grade student responses to Sunday school quizzes that were floating around on the Internet. I've picked a few items that humorously reflect the students misunderstanding of biblical people events and people.

Ancient Egypt was old. Gypsies and mummies who all wrote in hydraulics inhabited it. They lived in the Sarah Dessert. The climate of the Sarah is such that all inhabitants have to live elsewhere.

Moses led the Hebrew slaves to the Red Sea where they made unleavened bread, which is bread made without any ingredients. Moses went up on Mount Cyanide to get the ten commandos. He died before he ever reached Canada but the commandos made it.

Solomon had three hundred wives and seven hundred porcupines. He was an actual hysterical figure as well as being in the bible. It sounds like he was sort of busy too.

Unfortunately, such misinformation plagues people of all ages. You will also discover that Christianity is always enmeshed in creedal and doctrinal controversy. This results from the fact that Christians bear witness to an historical **Mystery** that demands our attempt to make sense of it. As strange as it may seem, all our efforts to interpret that **Mystery** results in some degree of failure. We always end up sanitizing or domesticating the **Mystery**. Both neuter the Mystery of the Jesus of Nazareth story. Nonetheless, a response of faith prompts us to seek to understand that **Mysterious** event. To put it another way, we can't make rational sense of it, but we have to try. And that's the big dilemma for Christians at all times and places.

In other words, our dilemma is complicated by the fact that we enter the mysterious world of the metaphysical when contemplating God, faith, death, and related issues. The metaphysical sphere is an eerie place beyond the grasp of our empirical senses. That means we can't feel, hear, see, taste, or smell anything that's in the metaphysical. We can only talk about that stuff, which is, for most people, the realm of *ghosties and ghoulies and long-legged beasties and things that go bump in the night*"[1] This eerie realm is scary stuff unless it's demystified, which is one of the goals of these letters.

---

1   This was supposedly part of an old 14th or 15th Century litany, probably Cornish, although my sources within the Anglican Church have not been able to locate it. The priest would say these words and the people would respond, "O, Lord deliver us!" If this was not part of an early post-Reformation litany "it should have been."

Don E. Post, Ph.D.

Since *religious issues* are rooted in this eerie realm most people get angry when issues are debated. Very angry! Belief differences have led to family feuds, caused people to leave one church for another, led to the establishment of totally new sects, and fueled many wars. Over the centuries Christians have consciously and deliberately killed hundreds of thousands who, for one reason or another, did not adhere to a predominant, taken-for-granted worldview.

My letters to you reflect thoughts developed over a lifetime of study and experience. I started my professional career as a Methodist minister, earning a master's degree in theology from Perkins School of Theology, Southern Methodist University, then a masters degree in sociology at Trinity University, and finally a doctor's degree in educational anthropology at the University of Texas. My theological reflections are shaped by education and personal life experiences— as all such views should be. Nonetheless, my beliefs are subject to revision when confronted by higher logic. And I hope I will always be a learner.

As you do your own reading and thinking in the years ahead, the following observations will hopefully provide you a mental trampoline—something to bounce off of as you develop your own understanding of the Sacred and its meaning for your life.

In matters of faith we all generally accept what parents, Sunday school teachers, or ministers tell us. That was certainly the story of my youth and early years in the ministry. Given the fact that, (a) such matters are non-scientific and un-testable by traditional scientific means, and (b) there seems to be such a wide range of Christian beliefs, and (c) the Christian literature is so vast that it is difficult to read everything, it's understandable that people are puzzled, uninterested, or smug when faced with the task of making sense of the Christian faith.

Over the years I've heard many people say, with a steely, defiant sneer, "Look, if it says in the Bible that two plus two equals nine, then that's what I believe!" At first blush it's easy to see how casually some Christians separate *faith* and *reason*. This doesn't need to be your story. First, don't accept any *hand-me-down* beliefs without analyzing each very, very carefully. Read extensively. And I've provided numerous reading suggestions throughout these letters. Second, don't put your mind in neutral when pondering issues of faith. There are no questions you should fear. Always be mentally honest. God doesn't ask any person to *dummy-up*. Only church organizations and religious fundamentalists tend to do that. Third, always remember two fundamental facts:

- God's love and acceptance of you does not depend upon what you believe,
- But…the *quality of your life* is entirely *dependent upon what you believe.*

You must keep these two issues completely distinct!

My Pilgrimage

Parts of my own pilgrimage may help you understand some of what you will encounter. Only in seminary was I introduced to Church history and the rich theological discussion of the last two thousand years. I was awe-struck.

As I look back on my youth I remember God as a macho-male figure, high in the sky in a fairyland called Heaven. God was *out there* or *up there*, depending upon whether one was lying or sitting. While he was remote on the one hand, he could, and did, come to earth and mete out rewards and punishments from time to time. He seemed to be responsible for all the good things that happened. But, interestingly, my elders relieved God of responsibility for the bad things that happen to people. As they did so, they dropped hints that led me to conclude that God would punish me if I didn't behave.

One went to Heaven if one believed in Jesus and didn't sin. There was no other way. Jesus, in turn, was this angelic, Anglo-Saxon Hollywood-type typified in Salmon's head of Christ painting. *Sin* had to do with smoking, drinking, cussing, lying, stealing, disobeying your parents, being unpatriotic, sexual behavior, and just being downright ornery. Being *saved* meant one was going to Heaven, but only if you shunned all the sins listed above—plus one had to go to church regularly, give money to the church, pray at meals, and read the Bible. Those were minimal expectations. Oh, and I should mention, laughter in religious spaces was frowned upon. If you giggled in church you got a spanking. I got lots of spankings.

As I grew older and learned to read and think it became obvious that what I had been taught, for the most part, was untrue. Unfortunately, what is still taught in church, regardless of denomination or sect, generally follows this simplistic line of thinking. Churches generally adhere to denominational party lines and follow a shallow, non-controversial theology.

Few bishops, priests, pastors, elders, Sunday school teachers, or others, are willing to question conventional religious folklore and be seen as controversial. Ministers try to be as non-controversial as possible for fear of losing parishioners. One has to be popular and keep the money rolling in. There's usually a large budget to support, so if too many members flee due to theological disagreements the minister will find himself in deep trouble. As any politician knows it is far more profitable to maintain a non-controversial posture.

And, of course, those who claim that every word written on the pages of a Bible is the *historically inerrant and scientific act of God* are always with us. I gradually realized that such views are signs of a weak faith. (This is also akin to the *flat-earth mentality.*) Admittedly not all ministers are fearful of the truth, but it's still a fairly common posture. And, the flip side of the coin is that there are members in most local churches who will leave in a huff if the minister challenges their childhood beliefs. In addition, many clergy believe people come to church to be inspired and not mentally challenged. So, the church moves on through the ages as a mighty army of soldiers armed with theological weaponry that wouldn't cut hot butter. In fact, much of it is so simple-minded, and often eerie, that it's embarrassing.

In the early stage of your pilgrimage you probably will find yourself puzzled by a number of things. For example, you will wonder, as I did, why Christian beliefs are controversial in the first place; why the Church killed so many during the Inquisition of the Middle Ages; why members of one church shun and abuse members of other churches; why Catholics and Protestants in Ireland kill each other; and why Christians and Muslims kill each other around this world? Isn't the Christian bunch supposed to be composed of people who love others in spite of their pimples?

These are thorny and often eerie issues. At the outset, without any *ifs*, *ands*, or *buts*, it's important that you *remember* my earlier admonition that

> *a person's relationship with the God of Jesus Christ is not dependent on right belief, creeds, or institutions.*

Instead, a relationship with the God of Jesus Christ is

> *an experiential phenomenon established by God and sustained by God that's grounded in the* **MYSTERIOUS** *historical life of Jesus Christ.*

The Apostle Paul stated that we are **justified by grace through faith in spite of the fact that we are all unacceptable** (*sinful, disobedient*). Notice the fact that we are unacceptable. That means that regardless of our beliefs, behaviors, attitudes, morality, or lack thereof, or anything else, *we are unacceptable to God*. **But he declared his love for us as unacceptable as we are.** This good news was further confirmed by the apostolic fathers during the first five centuries of the Church's life and emphasized again by the Protestant Reformers.

Although I will keep repeating this basic theological fact, it's important to remember that the phrase *in spite of the fact that we are all unacceptable* is essentially a summation of the New Testament message about the Christ manifest in and through the man Jesus; the core of Christianity. In other words,

> **in spite of our sin and guilt, unbelief, doubts, and total unworthiness, the fundamental miracle of the Christ event reveals God's acceptance of all of us** (even those we hate the most).

And God's acceptance of all humans, even Christian literalists, Christian (and Muslim) fundamentalists, Pentecostals, et. al, has nothing to do with right belief or right behavior, as much as that upsets many good, moralistic, pietistic, literalistic churchgoers! And this means that even though I view some preacher's apish, theatrical antics in the pulpit as total nonsense, I know that God's love and acceptance embraces him or her as much as it does me, mine and all others. It's important to stop with the preceding affirmations when summarizing the God-Man M**YSTERY**. That's all there is. Don't add anything else. (I will consistently use the phrase *God-Man* when referring to the life and death of Jesus of Nazareth because it represents the paradoxical dilemma as defined by the early Church.)

Once one accepts God's unconditional acceptance in and of itself, then one faces a totally new task. One must then ask, "What is a person's proper response to this magnificent gift of love?" In other words, keep a Christian lifestyle and the **salvation act** as found in the God-man M**YSTERY** separate. These are two different spheres.

What is a Christian's Life?

It has been my experience that everyone wants to define the Christian life, even those who are not Christian. In other words, how does one know a Christian from a non-Christian? And since this is such a critical issue I want to frame the answer for you in this very first letter.

Don E. Post, Ph.D.

Scripturally and historically a person who acknowledges God's love lives a life of **thanksgiving, humility,** and **loves other people (all people)**. Self-righteousness and elitist sentiments have no place in the life of any Christian. And notice also that I listed the love of <u>all</u> *others*. This is because the neighbor that Jesus often mentioned is **every** man, woman, and child on earth.

Unfortunately, too many of those who attach the Christian label to their self-identity may assent in church to the love of the neighbor, as per Jesus' command, but in practice reduce the neighbor to those (a) who agree with them or, (b) those who conform to their definition of right behavior. Others are shunned. I hope you don't follow this practice.

It's easy to test you're obedience to this NT litmus test. Check your reactions and feelings when you are face to face with a Muslim fundamentalist,…or a local bag lady,…or a gay person dying of AIDS,…a radical political activist,…a member of the Hell's Angels or Bandidos,…or a hair spiked, dyed bright orange, young man or woman, covered from head to feet with tattoos, with ear lobes, navel, lips, eye-lids, cheeks, and tongue pierced and laden with jewelry—and that's just a short list of one's possible encounters in our day and time. How we respect and care for those who are culturally different is the real test of our relationship with the God-Man Jesus.

Quite honestly, I've had a recurring nightmare about having my car horn stick while driving down the Interstate highway and look up to find that I'm right behind a gang of *Hell's Angels* motorcycles. And they're turning around giving me threatening looks!

You can be sure that knowing how to love the neighbor is not always easy or obvious. Besides my imaginary encounter with the Hell's Angels above, let me give you a more serious example—one that's faced by men and women on a recurring basis. Let's say that you find yourself in the U.S. military. As a soldier you find yourself armed and in combat. Finally, a young man that your superiors have defined as an enemy is in your gun sights. Is it an act of love to kill that person? He, like you, was placed in the kill or be-killed position by his government. What's God's will?

Yes, I am aware that nations depend upon their youth to protect them in times of war. Yes, I am aware that Jesus said, "Render unto Caesar…" etc. Nonetheless, every man and woman who responds to God's presence has to wrestle with this issue, or at least should. All people generally believe their nation's interest is

God's interest. During the Viet Nam War Christian Americans disagreed, often violently. What does it mean to love the neighbor in this context? Interestingly, you will find sensitive and authentic Christians on both sides of this issue. And you will find Christians on both sides of every controversial issue—abortion, use of contraceptives, the death penalty, and so forth.

What should you do in such situations? Simply put, you must wrestle with the ethics and make your decision and go on with your life. God loves you *no matter what you decide to do.* Authentic Christian life is not defined by social positions, but by **accepting God's love in humility and fearlessly struggling to act in love toward** *all others.*

Let me stress my point by using a *negative example.* Our local newspaper carried a story about a man and his family that was titled: "Practicing what he preaches: the hatred of homosexuals."[2] The man and his recruits reportedly go all over the country picketing churches and other groups who show any sympathy toward gays. The article states that the group even cheers at AIDS patient's funerals. They not only vilify gays, but Jews, and others who are culturally different. The leader of the group believes his hate is strictly in the service of God. This is an indication of how Scripture can be used to justify whatever evil humans create. Can *gas chambers* be far behind?

Why Are One's Beliefs Important?

Interestingly, among the high growth evangelical and Pentecostal mega churches that have sprouted across America in recent decades belief is unimportant. Recent research by sociologist Alan Wolfe, Director of the Boisi Center for Religion and American Public Life at Boston College, reveals that these conservative groups emphasize *experience* and not beliefs, tenets, or creeds.[3] In other words, to a growing mass of American Christians theology is unimportant.

I agree with their emphasis while disagreeing with de-emphasizing one's theological beliefs. It does reduce the demands placed on new members and makes it easier to attract new church members. But it's like throwing the baby out with the bath water.

---

2 "Practicing what he preaches: the hatred of homosexuals," in The Houston Chronicle, Sunday, December 15, 2002, p. 10A.

3 Wolfe, Alan, The Transformation of American Religion; How We Actually Live Our Faith, (New York: Free Press), 2003.

Don E. Post, Ph.D.

Although God's love for any person has nothing to do with his or her beliefs, one's beliefs comprise a mental map that guides one's attitudes and behaviors. The quality of one's life depends upon the beliefs one holds. To paraphrase the sociologist, W.I. Thomas, "If a people believe something to be true, it will be true in its effect." In other words, people act out of their beliefs. Let me give you some examples.

When I worked as a minister in San Antonio's inner city, some Mexicanos said that mothers scared their children with a tale of a headless horseman that roamed the streets at night. This tale, by the way, served the mothers needs to have their children in the house before dark. Interestingly, when I discussed this story with Mexicano adults and the laughter subsided, someone in the group would invariably say, "But I've met men who swear they have seen this headless horseman at night."

Did they really see a headless horseman? Most important, how does this belief affect a person's life? Obviously such a person sees the world as inhabited by *ghosties and ghoulies and long-legged beasties and things that go bump in the night*. Furthermore, if I see such a scary world it's doubtful I would be much of a risk taker. Second, the bad things that happen would be attributed to those *ghosties* and *ghoulies* out there, rather than to one's own bad judgments or random universal laws of nature. A life of fear is not a free and joyous life.

Interesting, isn't it? *Yes, the quality of one's life is affected by one's beliefs.*

A man named Jim Jones used scriptures to create a narrowly defined cult by attracting people who evidently had little understanding of the Christ event. Jones was a charismatic person and a dynamic speaker. His roots were in a mainline denomination. His interpretation of scripture gradually moved from basic Christian thought to a murky, paranoid interpretation of the faith conjured up in the deep recesses of his mind. He felt the presence of *ghosties and ghoulies and long-legged beasties and things that go bump in the night*. And because he couldn't explain them in traditional Christian terms, he used Scripture to create his own theological stew.

His followers had no way to judge the legitimacy of his claims. The end of that story is sad. In the early 1970s Jones led his followers to a four thousand acre tract in South America called Jonestown, Guyana. In 1978 they followed him in a mass suicide.

A shocking story. *Yes, the quality of life is affected by one's beliefs.*

A lady in Houston, Texas, named Andrea Yates drowned her five children because of beliefs she picked up from some quacky fundamentalist preacher that led her to think that Satan would torment them in Hell if she didn't. Obviously this is an extreme example, but it makes the point once again.

A tragic story. *Yes, the quality of life is affected by one's beliefs.*

People in a cult known as Heaven's Gate were so convinced this world was evil and dirty that they conjured up the idea to commit suicide so some extra-terrestrial craft could transport them to a far better place.

A sad story. *Yes, the quality of life is affected by one's beliefs.* Ahhh, the mind can do wonders as it weaves its worldviews!

Or think of fundamentalist Muslim believers who firmly believe they are God's chosen and all other people are infidels in need of extermination. The infidels in this case are non-Muslims, usually Westerners. This is a case where religious fundamentalism joins race and nationalism to forge an explosive mix. But pause in the midst of your feelings of revulsion to consider that we Christians have been eradicating those we consider infidels for centuries. There was the great Inquisition of the Middle Ages, the Salem witch trials, the massacre of Indians by the Spaniards at the time of the Conquest and by Anglo-American settlers in North America, to name a few of the most infamous cases.

Interestingly, many within Christianity believe God doles out laws, demands retribution for breaking any of those laws, and has an unsmiling, jealous, and vengeful demeanor. You will also find that such people are equally unsmiling, vengeful, and very authoritarian in their relationships with other people. It's interesting how one's beliefs about God shape not only one's worldview but also one's personality. Belief is a reflection of the inner-self. Or, to say it another way, thought shapes one's reality.

But, as important as beliefs are, never forget **that your beliefs do not buy or earn God's love and acceptance as expressed in Jesus Christ.** *The only immovable core belief in the Christian faith is that the God-Man was the Christ of history.* And this affirmation relies on the New Testament's compound that Jesus Christ was fully God and fully man. Once one moves beyond this core New Testament idea, historically the rest of the Church's doctrines are fluid. (By the way, the early Church beliefs were referred to as *dogma*. And the word *dogma* comes from the Greek word *dokein,* which originally referred to holding an opinion, having a judgment, doctrine, decree, or ordinance.[4])

Now that you've tucked away these essentials in your noggin, I want to suggest some ideas that should make your understanding of the Bible much clearer and more beneficial.

Biblical Literacy in the 21st Century

The Bible can be a formidable book to understand, but it doesn't have to be. The first part is called the Old Testament (it's really the Hebrew Bible) and contains stories about strange people that lived thousands of years ago in a far away land. (By the way, although one is the *Hebrew Bible* and the other the *Christian Bible*, I will follow convention and refer to them collectively as *the Bible* unless otherwise noted.)

People mentioned in the Bible often have some rather exotic names—like Ezekiel, Nebuchadnezzar, Melchizedek, and others. The second part is called the New Testament (it's really the Christian Bible) and it too contains stories. If some of these don't stun one's scientific, moral and psychic sensibilities one is probably brain dead. As you mature both the Hebrew and Christian Bibles will increasingly be the source of mystery and complexity.

The frustration will increase as you listen to all the various interpretations given to its content by an array of people. You will find that people can get pretty nasty when you don't agree with their interpretation of the scriptures. No one wants to discuss the Bible around others. Such anger is symptomatic of fear and lack of reliance on God's act in the God-Man MYSTERY. So, be forewarned.

Marcus Borg reminds us that the Bible is essentially a collection of stories.[5] He states that there are three features to the Biblical narratives.[6]

---

4 Joseph Henry Thayer, (Trans.), Greek-English Lexicon of the New Testament, (Edinburgh: T& T. Clark, 1956), p. 153f.
5 Marcus J. Borg, Meeting Jesus Again For the First Time, (San Francisco, CA:HarperCollins Publisher, 1995), p. 120f. It is always startling to be reminded of something so obvious!
6 Ibid.

There is the narrative framework of the Bible as a whole, which on a grand scale can be considered as a single story beginning with paradise lost in the opening chapters of Genesis, moving through the story of God's redeeming activity in Israel and through Jesus, and concluding with the vision of paradise restored in the final vision of the book of Revelation. The centrality of narrative…is also pointed to by the fact that it contains literally hundreds of individual stories. And, finally, at the center of Scripture are a small number of "macro-stories"—the primary stories that shaped the religious imagination and life of ancient Israel and the early Christian movement.

So there you have a biblical synopsis of sorts.

Stories are powerful means of communication because they can carry a myriad of meanings, truisms, and insights. Biblical stories have been told and retold for many centuries and never lose their ability to resonate at the deepest level of human existence.

In addition, Borg believes three stories shape the Biblical drama as a whole, while each maintains its unique perspective of the religious life. He states:

Two of the stories are grounded in the history of ancient Israel: the story of the exodus from Egypt, and the story of the exile and return from Babylon. The third, the priestly story, is grounded…in an institution—namely, the temple, priesthood, and sacrifice.[7]

An understanding of these stories is crucial for understanding the New Testament for they comprised the backdrop imagery for what's communicated in this later phase. Understandably, once this is all said, the task of coming to grips with the Bible is still a challenge.

Language: A Formidable Problem in Christianity

In the midst of it all keep a cool head and realize that it's impossible for anyone to understand *everything* Biblical. Don't despair. Know that the original books of the Bible were written in Hebrew, Aramaic, and Greek. Incredibly, some people still don't understand the implications of this fact. Translating words from one language to another is difficult at best. And the Bibles have been

---

7   Borg, Op. Cit., p. 121f.

through dozens of translations. In the case of early translations those doing the work had no qualms about making sure their linguistic changes fit their own cultural views. Our problem with the Biblical language is of significant proportion. One scholar emphasized this problem by stating:

> Language that conceals rather than reveals, that obstructs rather than constructs, is a problem. It is out of time, out of place, out of rhythm. Much of the Language of the New Testament has become problematic in this sense.[8]

Remember, language is a living thing. People of every age constantly add new words, give existing words new meanings, borrow words from their neighbors, and so forth. We have to rely on existing limitations even as scholars continue to search for clearer translations. But even as we struggle with language we do so with the knowledge that...

- the Mystery of Christ is the Mystery of God in action and
- we can say nothing literal because all our language about God's mysterious act in Jesus Christ is beyond any human literalization or language.

This may sound discouraging, but we have no other choice. Language is our most important means of communication. And once the Jesus event historically ended those early witnesses were immediately challenged to make sense of it. They had to interpret it to themselves and then to others. And so it has always been. Every generation wrestles with the interpretive task within Christianity, even though it ultimately escapes our attempts.

The King James Version (KIV) of the Bible (published version in 1539 C.E. then revised in 1611) was the most widely used version in America until the Revised Standard Version (RSV) hit the streets right after World War II.[9] The RSV built on work previously done by scholars in England back in the 1880's. To Church leaders and Biblical scholars the fact that the English language had undergone such tremendous change necessitated a more understandable

---

8   Robert W. Funk, <u>Parables and Presence: Forms of the New Testament Tradition</u>, (Philadelphia: Fortress Press, 1982), p. 15.

9   See a comprehensive listing and discussion of the various translations in Henry Snyder Gehman (ed.), <u>The New Westminster Dictionary of the Bible</u>, (Philadelphia: The Westminster Press, 1970, p. 971f; and the fine work by the Jesus Seminar group in Robert W. Funk, Roy W. Hoover, and the Jesus Seminar, <u>The Five Gospels</u>, (San Francisco: HaperCollinsPublishers, 1993), p. xiiif.

translation for our time. Many of the words and phrases in the King James Version were no longer understood, even though most churchgoers were used to hearing them. Scholars had also discovered older manuscripts that clarified a number of translating problems.

All of this didn't matter to a large number of Americans who had grown up with the King James Version and didn't want to change. I received some criticism when I read from the new Revised Version in my little country churches back in 1955-6. And the RSV was a modest revision of the KJV!

There's an oft-told story about a lady who got angry when her preacher used the Revised Standard Version one Sunday. She screamed at her preacher, "If the King James [version] wuz good 'nuf for Jesus, it's gud 'nuf fer me!"

Yes, indeed. Meanwhile, Biblical scholars have been studying the original Aramaic, Hebrew, and Greek texts for centuries and still argue over much of it. But you, like most, are not going to learn these exotic languages in order to read the original Biblical manuscripts, although it would certainly enhance your life. Until that time the English versions will suffice. You have to learn to ignore people who, for some strange misguided reason believe God wrote the thing.

To be intellectually honest read both Bibles with a clear understanding that the linguistic vehicles for communicating what is ultimately the *incommunicable Mystery of God* are aphorisms, allegories, myths, poetry, metaphors, parables, and other such devices. Don't fall into the trap of reading the scripture as scientific reports! You can't literalize the God-Man M**YSTERY**. As we say in the south, *that dog won't hunt!* (I'll discuss this further in other letters.)

I hope the following comments help simplify your task of understanding both the Hebrew and the Christian Bibles, because it's important that you engage these works in a serious manner.

Choosing One's Drain

A minister friend once said "Life is the process of dying and we all go down one drain or another in life." It's important to *choose that drain wisely.*

That may seem like a crude way of talking about life and death, but it's an appropriate metaphor for our human dilemma. Every man and woman makes a choice regarding the ultimate meaning of life. Each chooses, whether *off the shelf* or *self-created*, a basic meaning of life that drives all their actions. No one can live life without being driven by some ultimate worldview. Each of us dies having *bet their life on that choice*. The Christian Faith is one *drain* among many.

The story of Jesus is a *drain choice* that claims God reconciled the world to Himself. To accept this Mystery as the defining meaning of one's life is said to restore one to authentic humanity. In other words, one is loved and accepted by the God of history and the acceptance of God's love frees one to live in celebration.

Those who have chosen the God-Man Mystery as their *drain* claim that the decision totally transformed their life. Where they were once miserable, they are now joyous, where life had been a burden, it is now celebratory, and so forth. All together, not a bad *drain* to go down!

Thomas Jefferson said, "I have sworn upon the altar of God eternal hostility against every form of tyranny over the mind."

The belief that the world teems with *ghosties and ghoulies and long-legged beasties and things that go bump in the night* is one of the most tyrannical forces to haunt anyone. My next letter is a further step in eliminating these demons from a contemporary Christian worldview.

SECOND LETTER

THE BIBLE: MAGIC, MYSTICISM OR FAITH

Dear Ben and Grace,

In order to develop a meaningful understanding of the Christian faith it's important that you know how to read the Bible. Most people fall victim to a number of traps that prevent them from appreciating the vast riches of the Biblical works. I hope my experiences  will save you agonizing encounters with some of these *ghosties, ghoulies and long-legged beasties* that others have encountered.

Let me first redefine the concept of *myth*. People generally think of *myth* as a statement or story that's untrue, like a fairy-tale. On the other hand, in the anthropological discipline *myth* refers to the *meanings* or *images* in the heads of a particular people, a cultural set of ideas. Although in this usage *myth* is a value, preference, idea, or concept, it has nothing to do with truth or untruth. *Worldviews* are *myths* (ideas, concepts) stored in the minds of a people that define reality. Every person constantly tests the truth, veracity or usefulness of his or her worldviews. We can say, for example, that the current scientific worldview is *a mythic idea* by which millions of today's people view, define, and respond to their world. Crop circles, UFOs, and *end of the world schemes* (dispensationalism) pose problems for many who apply the scientific worldview in most areas of their lives. As strange as it may seem, not all people in this world possess and use *the scientific myth* in their daily lives, so the world looks different to them. And, as I noted earlier, religious fundamentalists are increasingly annoyed, if not deeply fearful, of the scientific worldview's creation of modernity.

Second, it's important to clarify the ideological difference between the political and/or religious *right* and *left*. I personally find these to be annoying terms because they are used as weapons in order to typify people. People are far more diverse than such polarizing labels suggest. Unfortunately, too many people use one label or another because *their peer group does*. Invariably those who hurl these labels don't understand the real meaning of the terms. The critical difference between the religious and/or political *right* and *left* revolves around the concept of "being human."[10] Both extremes pervert our humanness. Both the *right* and the *left* reduce life's ambiguity. The *right* by hawking the notion of *fate* and the *left by pushing* the idea of absolute *freedom*. The *fated right* position looks to the future through a rear-view mirror as it seeks Eden in some imagined golden age. They view social change as the work of satanic influences. Hence, *moderns* (most Westerners) are demons. The extreme *left*, on the other hand, sees no redeeming value in anything of the past. Both extremes sell half-truths.

It's closer to the truth to say that each human is a socio-cultural product and carries all that respective cultural baggage. This is an immutable and inescapable fact of human life. It is our *fate*. There are no options at this level. But each person is gifted with the ability to make an enormous array of decisions about life. Each person can create the future, which includes taking a position about the past, the socially and physically inherited baggage, and so forth. Obviously some are freer than others. Some have a greater array of options. Moderns, for example, have a greater range of choices than traditional peoples.

In contemporary terms, to be human means to live in the ambiguity of having the *past* pulling one way and *freedom's urge to create* pulling another. Every person is trapped in this tension. Religious fundamentalists either deny modernity, try to repeal modernity through the exercise of political activism, or take up a gun. *Leftists* either opt out of the social system or take up the gun. Both extreme views are deeply flawed. At the current time, however, the world's religious fundamentalists are dishing out death, destruction, intolerance, and hate.

---

10   Averill, Lloyd J. Religious Right, Religious Wrong, (New York: The Pilgrim Press, 1989).

My task at hand has nothing to do with the Koran, but everything to do with the Judeo-Christian tradition. With the preceding in mind, let's clarify the nature of the Bible.

First, you will discover that some people view the Bible as a *mystical* or *magical book*[11] that contains the rules for human behavior. And there are those, as I said earlier, who believe God wrote every single, solitary word. The Bible to these folks was a *Godly transcription*. Not true. You will also find people who view the Bible as good literature.

Please note that the Bible is not, (a) a magical item, (b) a compendium of rules for proper behavior, (c) just good literature, and (d) although we might agree the various books and letters were *inspired*, it was not written by God.

We can dispense with the first illusion by emphasizing that the Bible is an object in space and time. Like other books it is composed of paper and ink. The cover may be of some type of stiff matter, leather, or some other exotic material, but it's still papers covered with ink-imprinted words.

Now this may seem so elementary as to be ridiculous, but you'd be surprised at the number of people who don't grasp this fact. The Bible is not imbued with mystical or magical properties. In other words, you can sleep on it, but it won't heal your migraines or remove your stress and anxiety. In fact, you may wake up with a crick in your neck or a headache. You are free to mark passages of scripture that mean the most to you or make notes in the margins. That's not sacrilegious. It's paper, for goodness sake.

Second, although the advice given between its covers is sometimes, but not always, of the highest moral order, the Bible is not a *Christian's* encyclopedia of behavioral rules. It is not a set of *dos* and *don'ts* for proper behavior. Many Christians search the Scriptures to find out what they should do in particular situations. At first blush this is not necessarily a bad idea, since there are worse places one can go. But it's misguided. (Jesus had problems with the manner in

---

11   Following the anthropologist Bronislaw Malinowski, magic refers to an expressive symbolism that serves a cathartic need as it functions to relieve an individual of stress, tension or anxiety. In reference to the Bible, people might tend to view it as having some degree of mystical or metaphysical powers of its own. Practitioners are as scientific in their views as their technology allows. See, Malinowski, B. Magic, Science and Religion, (Garden City, NY: Doubleday, 1948).

which his fellow Hebrews misinterpreted the Jewish scripture, which allowed them to abuse the purity laws.)

It has been my experience that people tend to use scripture to support their point of view when they want to humiliate another. Using Scripture as a means of winning an argument is the extreme tactic of one-upmanship. It's also akin to shaking a believed mystical or magical item in one's face and crying out, "Ahaaa, God is goin' a git ya now, you pervert you, cuz you don't believe like me!" Again, that's an abuse of the scriptures. There's more than a little voodoo in all this. As Shakespeare noted, "The Devil can cite Scripture for his purpose."[12]

The rules and ethical admonitions found in the scriptures were written for people living in a specific culture at a specific time. For the most part the biblical injunctions, or laws, don't fit our cultural environment. One can find scripture to support about any act you so desire. Conversely, one can find scripture to trounce behavior you don't agree with. It's a great weapon. If you want to denounce homosexuality, quote scripture. If you want to denounce interracial marriage, quote scripture. If you want to denounce musical instruments in church, quote scripture. If you want to denounce dancing, quote scripture. Conversely, if you want to support killing, quote scripture. If you want to support the superiority of the white, Anglo race, quote scripture. And on and on it can go. This is total nonsense!

If you want further proof of how ridiculous biblical literalism can be, pretend that a man owes another man a million dollars and has been paying that back for over six years without missing a payment. Then, at the end of the seventh year he says to his creditor that his debt should be canceled because it says so in the Bible. Sure enough, in Deuteronomy 15 men are told to forgive all debts at the end of the seventh year. That sounds good to me! But I don't know any Westerners who would accept that today. Capitalism would be in a mess!

The Hebrew Bible also speaks of women as *men's property*. Daughters were stoned to death if their commercial value was damaged by their loss of virginity (Deut. 22:20f; Exod. 21:1f; and, Num. 31:18). I believe some of the latest American studies indicate that approximately thirty to forty percent of young, unmarried women professed to having had sexual activity prior to marriage. Uhmmm, if we really took this Old Testament law seriously every town in

---

12   Shakespeare, I, iii, 99.

America would have daily stonings. Why don't we stone these gals today? Where's the faith in the Bible?

Where's faith, indeed! There are so many other inapplicable laws and admonitions in the Bible that could be trotted out that it boggles the mind to think of any sane person adhering to a literalistic interpretation of the scriptures. It's always been interesting to me to find that those who claim such devotion to biblical law only reference those laws they agree with. I've also wondered why the texts such biblical commandos adore so much are those that hammer their neighbors and never themselves?

The emphasis on scripture started with the Protestant Reformation's emphasis on *Sola Scriptura* [scripture alone] as the only witness a person needs in the faith. Unfortunately, as Martin Marty suggests (quoting Jaroslav Pelikan and Albert Outler), the Scriptures have never been *sola*:

> Give a basic New Testament passage to an Orthodox, a Lutheran, a Calvinist, an Anglican, and a Congregationalist to interpret—and the discrepancies in their interpretation will correlate much too closely with the various historically conditioned traditions in which they stand to justify any claim that they did no more than reproduce the original meaning.[13]

This, by the way, includes all of us, Baptists, Methodists, Pentecostals, or whatever. **Our interpretation of Scripture is filtered through our institutional history, culture, psychic composition, and life experiences.**

Let me hastily add that Jesus, as a Jew and probably a Pharisee, looked upon the law as Yahweh's blueprint for human behavior. Jesus certainly held the Jewish scriptures in deep reverence, but he certainly did not see them as *inerrant*. He reportedly departed from a great deal of Jewish scriptural tradition by saying, "You have heard that it was said to the men of old...But I say to you..." His mission focused on the abuse of the Judaic law. As Borg so aptly states, Jesus attacked the prevailing *purity system*, a life circumscribed by purity rules, in order to establish "a community shaped by the ethos and politics of compassion."[14]

---

13 Marty, Martin <u>A Short History of Christianity,</u> (Philadelphia: Fortress Press, 1987), p. 165f.
14 Borg., <u>Op. Cit.</u>, p. 52f.

For example, Jesus supposedly questioned the tradition of fasting (Mark 2:18f), the ban on picking grain on the Sabbath (Mark 3:20f), eating with defiled hands (Mark 7:1f), and so on. Time and again Jesus reportedly revealed the outrageous abuse of the law by the self-righteous. The following comprise a few of his invectives that provide us insight into Jesus' attitude toward the law—and love of God and compassion toward all others:[15]

You scholars and Pharisees, you imposters! Damn you! You pay tithes on mint and dill and cumin too, but ignore the really important matters of the Law, such as justice and mercy and trust. You should have attended to the last, without ignoring the first. You blind leaders! You strain out a gnat and gulp down a camel.[16]

Or again,

Isaiah was right when he prophesied about you hypocrites, as it is written:

These people honor me
with their lips,
but their hearts are far from me,

They worship me in vain;
Their teachings are but rules
Taught by men.[17]

You have let go of the commands of God and are holding on to the traditions of men.

It is evident that over time many in Judaism had abused the law to the point that it had become the problem instead of the solution. Jesus continues blistering the law abusers in the Gospel of Mark (the earliest Gospel) by saying that nothing that goes into a man can make him impure or unclean. It is what comes out of a man that can be evil. And he clearly specified that it was the things *coming out of men* that are impure or evil:

---

15 Funk & Hoover, Op. Cit., p. 242.
16 Matthew 23:23f. Of these words, the Jesus Seminar scholars generally agreed that Jesus might have said the words in verse 24.
17 Isaiah 29:13

What comes out of a man is what makes him unclean. For from within, out of men's hearts, come evil thoughts, sexual immorality, theft, murder, adultery, greed, malice, deceit, lewdness, envy, slander, arrogance and folly. All these evils come from inside and make a man unclean.[18]

I could go on with this line of thought, but you can read the words attributed to Jesus and see how the aphorisms, allegories, metaphors, and parables attacked and undermined the prevailing misinterpretation of Jewish scripture, abuse of the law, or the purity system.

Yes, Jesus believed in the law as applicable in his time, but he saw it as subservient to loving God and one's neighbor. Furthermore, we don't want to paint all Judaism as populated by Pharisaical tyrants, as Borg so aptly admonishes.[19] Unfortunately, we have a tendency to over-generalize when thinking about past ages and people who can't defend themselves. Nor is it fair to characterize the God of the Old Testament as strictly wrathful, vengeful, and judgmental. He was occasionally characterized as loving, forgiving, and compassionate. Jesus' God was such a *compassionate God.*

Every age has its moralists who adhere to an abusive *purity system*. Such people are sprinkled throughout every congregation. It gets absurd. Some claim it's evil to have musical instruments in the church, for women to use cosmetics, for anyone to cuss, smoke, drink beer and/or liquor, dance, and so forth. Traditionally it has been said that one should not associate with those who do any or all these things; and yada, yada, yada. By the way, Jesus was heavily criticized for enjoying the company of ne'er do wells.

Modern day American moralists populate the *Church of the Can't and Shan't Doers*. These modern day, self-righteous biblical commandos, ignoring Jesus' impassioned plea to love one another, have taken bits and pieces from the Hebrew Bible, mixed in some key American culture traits, and come up with a *Christus Americanus*, or *American Christ*. This is a concoction that is totally antithetical to the *kerygmatic*[20] Jesus.

---

18   Mark 7:20f. The Jesus Seminar biblical scholars were unanimous in their opinion that Jesus didn't utter these words. Nonetheless, they are part of that early oral tradition and maintain the tenor of Jesus' message.
19   Borg, Op. Cit., p. 78.
20   From the Greek noun Kerygma and generally refers to the earliest theological meaning of Jesus' life and death. See Van A. Harvey, A Handbook of Theological Terms, (New York: The MacMillan Company), p. 138f.

Remember, using the Bible to search out rules and laws for every single modern day dilemma or to use the law as a litmus test for deciding who is Christian or to abuse another, *is not* the proper Christian approach to understand the Biblical literature.

Early on in my ministry an elderly retired Presbyterian minister asked me if I were familiar with the text in Matthew 7:16 that says, "By their fruits ye shall know them." Of course I probably nodded that I did, but probably didn't. I vividly remember his long bony finger waggling in my face as he sternly admonished me, saying, "But always remember that God didn't appoint you to be a fruit inspector!"

Scholars warn of reading the Christian Bible and finding a Jesus entirely congenial to one's own cultural worldview.[21] But I'll come back to all this later.

It should hastily be added that a Christian's freedom from the law should *not* be interpreted as the freedom to act immorally or licentiously![22] Quite the opposite. The full Christian equation should be stated as, *freedom from the law leads to the freedom of responsibility for the neighbor.*

One final word about the dangers of using the Bible as an encyclopedia. Not only is it *not a moral rulebook*, it *is not a scientific fact book*. In addition to the flat earth people I mentioned earlier, there are people in the 21st Century who take literally the Bible's account of creation, they seem to be unfamiliar with the fact that there are *two versions*. They fight scientific evolutionism with a zeal that would make those who participated in the European Inquisition blush with envy. They are book burners and, if the law would allow, probably heretic burners!

Third, although the Bible includes some great literature and history, it is more than that. To believers it is a record of God's relationship to humankind, written by the faithful through the eyes of faith.

Fourth, God did not write the Bible. God does not speak a particular language. And I know this will bother a lot of Americans who, through some weird fantasy, believe Jesus not only spoke English, but he was a red, white, and blue American. (By the way, many Republicans believe Jesus was a Republican! And

---

21   Funk & Hoover, <u>Op. Cit.,</u> p. 5.
22   Read Martin Luther's, <u>Treatise on Christian Liberty</u>. It's still in print.

some Democrats swear he was a Democrat. Nothing can shake such sterling ideology. One can only wonder what drives people to such quirky conclusions.)

You will often hear the Bible referred to as *the Word of God*. That's not *really* what our Protestant Reformation tradition says. What Luther and others maintained is that the <u>Word</u> of God is <u>in</u> the Bible. Or, one can say that *in* the Bible there <u>is the Word</u> *of God*. The writer of the gospel of John states that,

> In the beginning was the Word (Logos), and the Word (Logos) was with God, And the Word (Logos) was God.[23]

So "the Word" does not refer to the *words* of either the Hebrew or Christian Bibles, but the spiritual presence of the *I am who I am* that reveals himself through those narratives. In a later letter I will discuss the Greek notion of *Logos*, which was adopted by the early Christians as a means of talking about the Christ.

For now it is important that you distinguish between a word written on the pages of the Bible versus the Word that is revealed in the Bible witness. Notice that when I use **Word** (**Logos**) as synonymous with the divine I've put it in bold print and capitalized it. When I don't, as in word with a little *w*, I am referring to human language.

Summarily, the people who wrote the biblical documents were believers reporting events or expounding in praise of their God through the *eyes of faith*. In the same way we believe that God influences a minister's sermon or a Sunday school teacher's lesson. Certainly we don't blame God for all the contradictions and misunderstandings one finds in sermons—or scripture. To construct a faithful interpretation (theology) of the God-Man **Mystery** you must remember that the purpose of Scripture has always been to reveal the *Mysterious God-Man-Christ*. **Don't confuse "The Word" with "the words."**

Christian testimonies to the God-Man **Mystery** are presented in many ways and with varying adornments. Yet, there is a common thread to all such biblical testimonies: *in Jesus God reconciled the world to Himself.*

---

23   John 1:1

But making sense of these ancient documents has always been a problem for later generations. When men began to take the highly symbolic oral tradition and put it into Aramaic, Hebrew, and Greek, there was bad and good news. The bad news was that we shifted gears from trying to understand a *word from* God to trying to understand *a word about* God, which restates what I had said earlier. There's a big difference in these two perspectives.

A word *from* God has to do with God speaking to man, while a word *about* God has to do with what men say about God.[24] The good news was that the written tradition could be handed out and people could study it, which has the effect of providing a more fertile environment for God to be present in a human encounter.

This may seem like splitting hairs, but bear with me. We're back to the business of distinguishing *Word* from *word* once again, but at a low level of conceptualization.

- First, a *word from* God is the *Word* in the present tense. It is a personal word to an individual man or woman in present time. If one pays attention to that *Voice* that is always speaking to each of us, it is the *Word (God)* that creates faith.
- Second, the *word* about God from other men comes to us as a demand, and that word does not create faith, although such verbiage can put one into a preparatory state. Furthermore, the *word* about God is almost invariably sullied and distorted with the speaker's own cultural impediments. But finally *only God, directly speaking to each human, creates faith.*

The sum total of this dilemma between God speaking *to us* and other men speaking *about* God through their testimony as recorded in the Bible suggests that one has to clearly distinguish the difference between the two voices. And as I stated earlier, preaching and teaching in any age is a similar revelatory activity.

My next letter will show how our contemporary worldview differs from that of the early Christians and what a profound distinction this makes in our faith.

---

24 I don't remember where this came from. It's not an original distinction of mine. It could have come from Walter Wink, Engaging the Powers, (Minneapolis, Minn: Fortress Pres, 1992), Marcus Borg, Paul Tillich, or any number of sources.

THIRD LETTER

THE EARLY HEBREWS & CHRISTIANS

Dear Ben and Grace:

Now that you have a grasp of some issues associated with understanding the biblical literature, let's look at the people who recorded the biblical stories. You must learn to appreciate how differently they saw the world than we do in the 21st Century.

The biblical record is rooted in the life of a Semitic linguistic family of Arabian origin inhabiting an area of what is now called the Middle East several thousand years before the birth of Jesus of Nazareth (Arabs and Jews). As I stated in the beginning, these people will seem strange to you. As I write our nation is involved in a war against people in the Middle East that we've labeled as *terrorists*, and given the media discussions, it's clear that we don't understand either the Muslin terrorist's worldview or that of Arabs in general. Given our general level of cross-cultural ignorance of Mid-Easterners in the Twenty First Century, how can we claim to understand their ancestors who lived thousands of years ago?

The Ancient Worldview

Understanding begins by admitting that those early Hebrew's *worldview was totally different than ours—and still is.* For one thing, they believed the world to be flat, not round or oval, and it was three-storied. They gazed up at the sky and believed a canopy held the water back and stored snow and hail.[25] The sky's canopy was supported by pillars. In their view, God (Yahweh, Adonai, Elohim), resided *out there* in deep space. Further, if one dug into the earth deep enough one would find *Sheol*, the *abode of the dead*. This underworld contained a fountain and rivers. If you haven't already thought about it, this is the reason so many people today still think of God as *out there* and satanic forces as *down there*.

Today we know better, even if we don't act like it. We now conceptualize the God revealed through the Christian Scriptures as *within us, within our neighbors, and all around us,* not *out there*.

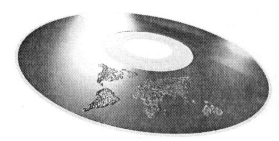

A Flat Earth Schema[26]

By the way, and you better be sitting down for this bit of news, some people in the world today still believe the earth is flat! And many are westerners. You can find their web sites on the Internet. That's pretty scary. I've met a few flat earth people, but they weren't westerners. Back in the late 1960s I was part of a team from the University of Texas doing research in Guatemala.

One of our analytical tasks depended on getting blood samples from local Maya in the village (municipio) of San Antonio Ilotanengo, Quiche. They believed the world to be flat. They had heard that some Americans had recently landed on the moon and since that event there had been greater rainfall than usual in the mountains of Guatemala. The rumor spread among the Maya that the astronauts had tinkered around with the sky canopy and it was now leaking. They were upset with us, to say the least.

Although this boggles our Western minds, it indicates how different people's minds can be. Or to put it in social science lingo, it shows how reality is *socially constructed*. Our minds are not blotters, soaking up an exact replica of everything we experience by our senses that's out there. We take in, filter, and

---

25 *Interpreter's Dictionary of the Bible,* (Nashville, Tnn: Abingdon Press, Vol. I), p. 703.
26 Used by permission of artist, Jarn Louiscash-Gary

then interpret what we see and experience through our culturally given worldviews. A culturally learned set of worldviews is all the reality any human has—at any time and place. Pioneers, those with new ideas regarding what's real, are rarely appreciated. In fact, those stalwart Christian leaders of the 15th, 16th and 17th centuries did not appreciate the scientific revelations of their newly emerging scientists. Copernicus (1473-1543) and Galileo (1564-1642) were abused for claiming that the sun was the center of the universe and the earth but one of many planets that revolved around it.

Moonrise[27]

Therefore, don't be amazed at the variety of religious views you run into in your lifetime. You may not yet understand the fact that *reality is socially constructed,* but you should. It is always amazing to see what people can create in their minds, from alligator gods to *Voodoo,* to modern notions that little space ships are coming to take the faithful to a home faraway! But, and this is critical, God's love and acceptance extends even to kooky people with weird worldviews, even flat-earthers and voodooers. There are no exceptions.

But getting back to the early Hebrews, they were a tribally organized people who gathered food from the river deltas and herded their animals across the sparsely grassed plains. They competed for food and grazing land with other Semitic tribal people of the area, such as the Phoenicians. Yet, they were influenced by the neighboring great cultures of Egypt and Mesopotamia and practiced polytheism (the worship of many gods) during their early years.

Eventually a group of these nomadic herders and gatherers became known as Israelites. They were still polytheistic. Weird acting men showed up from time to time and were called Prophets. They were weird because they looked and acted out-of-the-ordinary. Some Hebrews eventually persuaded a minority to worship one god (monotheism), whom they named Yahweh.

By the way, all tribes and groups of people have had strange people crop up in their midst. The stranger the behavior of these people, the more everyone thought they were possessed by spirits—some evil, some good. Shamen, or

---

27   NASA

what we've historically called *witch doctors*, were of this ilk. Either way, people watched these strange people for signs from the gods. Today we put weird people in mental institutions, while humorously tolerating others. Some become entertainers and TV evangelists!

Monotheism did not catch on as a dominant force among the early Hebrews until a few centuries before the birth of Jesus of Nazareth. The getting there was difficult. The Israelites fought, bickered, and squabbled among themselves and with neighboring tribes. To make a long story short, out of all this conflict eventually emerged a tribe within Israel started by a man called Judah, one of Jacob's sons. Judah's family eventually split into five tribal families, which proceeded from his three sons and three grandsons. Although initially commanding a minority of the Israelites, Judah's ideas of God ultimately captured the allegiance of the majority of people and their practices and beliefs were came to be known as *Judaism*.

It will help if you understand that there are two pivotal, or defining moments in Israel's life as reported in the Hebrew Bible.[28] There was the (1) exodus from Egypt and (2) the exile and return from Babylon. These are stories of bondage and liberation. In both cases, the Hebrew people *interpret* their bondage as a result of unfaithfulness to God and the subsequent liberation as an act of God's love. Human bondage, and the consequent alienation from God, represents the human condition that I will discuss in more detail in a future letter. Liberation has to do with salvation.

Hebrew priests spoke of man's relationship to God in terms of sin, guilt, and restoration (salvation) through sacrificial acts. Sinfulness was equated with being dirty, impure, and defiled. Priestly acts were to cleanse one from all this dirtiness in order to make one pure and acceptable to God. Hence the development of the *purity laws*.

As important as these pivotal stories are, there's a bit you should understand that prepared the Hebrews for their experiences in bondage. Judaists viewed themselves as uniquely favored by God, whom they held accountable for creating the universe. God created man in his own image.[29] (Interestingly, most

---

28 Borg, Op. Cit., p. 121f., speaks of these two events as "stories."
29 Biblically the notion of man refers to both genders (male and female). See Genesis creation stories, where "God created man, male and female..."

primitive people believe they are the Creator's special people.) Judaists believed that man rebelled (Sin) against God at the very beginning, which led to the present state of *alienation* between God and man.

Judaism further insisted that in spite of man's Sin (rebellion) God still loved his people. So God, they claimed, chose a man named Abraham to form a nation of people who would be loyal to Him. They further believed that God made a covenant, or bond, with Abraham that extended to all his descendants. That meant that Abraham and his descendants would be God's people *if*, and only *if*, they did as he said and obeyed His laws and observed the proper rituals. Circumcision was the universal sign of this covenant. Now parents all over the world, regardless of their faith, have their sons circumcised for health reasons, which points out how a religious trait can eventually be disconnected from its origin.

The Hebrew Law

The Law, or Pentateuch, is summed up in the Torah, which is the Hebrew name for the first five books of the Hebrew Bible.[30]

The Torah Scrolls

The core of the Torah is the Ten Commandments (a.k.a Decalogue) found in Exodus 20 and Deuteronomy 5, but all the purity laws are also found there. Many of the Torah's provisions antedate Moses.[31] Exodus 20 is the older form. The primary difference between these two versions is that the Sabbath is cited as a day of rest in the earlier, since God supposedly created the universe in six days and rested on the seventh. In the later version the Sabbath is highlighted as a day of remembrance for God's delivering Israel from Egyptian captivity.

---

30   Henry Snyder Gehman (ed), The New Westminster Dictionary of the Bible, (Philadelphia: Westminster Press, 1970), p. 727.
31   Ibid., p. 935.

In addition, the Pentateuch includes enormous regulations on food, diet, and ritual observances. There are a hundreds of them. In fact, there are so many that it's doubtful any human being could observe them all—at all times and in all places.[32] As I noted earlier, all these purity law were appropriate for tribal people living during those centuries, but most are not applicable in modern times. It's important to understand how forcefully the purity laws structured early Hebrew society. Although all societies are socially stratified, some are more stratified than others. In other words, people are always thrown into social categories or classes. Priests were at the top of the social heap in Judaic society and were supposed to be descendents of the founding families—Levi, Aaron, et. al.. In other words, the priesthood was a hereditary category. One couldn't earn one's way into the priesthood. Those who were Israelites by birth comprised the second highest class and converts to Judaism were third. Outcasts—all people with physical defects—were the lowest social class.

The Judaic class structure was further complicated by observance of the purity laws. The *pure* versus the *impure* became a basic social fault line in early Hebrew society. The pure were the *righteous* and the impure were the *sinners*. The righteous were all those who kept the purity laws. The sinners were those who didn't, plus a whole legion of physically disabled—lepers, eunuchs, the sick and lame. Those physically ailing were thrown into the category of sinners because it was thought their ailments were God's direct punishment. (Unfortunately, many Christians and Jews still believe this.)

Joining the physically disabled and those who lacked the requisite hereditary credentials to be among the elite were the economically poor, women, and gentiles. Poorness was also seen as a sign of God's punishment, and still seems to be for some in America. Femaleness had generally been viewed by the Hebrews as a second rate condition, and that's also a prevalent social perception today. Obviously the gentile, or non-Jew, was unclean and sinful.

In addition to these social categories, there were a number of religious sects during Jesus' lifetime that stood out. In fact, there is some scholarly support for the notion that Jesus was a member of that most influential group known as the Pharisees. The Sadducees and the Essenes were the other two main parties in town. The Pharisees believed in the immortality of the soul, the resurrection of the body, the existence of angels and spirits, that we are rewarded or punished

---

32   Read Deuteronomy to get a flavor of how detailed, ponderous, and culturally specific the law was.

after death, that the souls of evil people shall be kept in a hellish type holding facility under the earth somewhere (sheol), and the good and righteous will pass into a new body and continue to live. That sums up the key points of their beliefs. [The scribes, to whom you will be introduced as you read the Christian Bible, were Pharisees who had expertise in the law.]

The effect of the purity laws upon Hebrew society was the development of what the social sciences characterize as a very closed social system. Social boundaries were clear and formidable. There was no ambiguity. One trespassed these purity social boundaries at great risk. One stayed on one's side of the tracks!

It is obvious from comments by Jesus, Paul, and other early church leaders that obedience to the law leads to a virulent infection called *self-righteousness*." I'll continue to mention this fact throughout my letters because the human mind seems predisposed to forget this danger. Sometimes the infection of self-righteousness got so bad that the bulk of ordinary people suffered greatly. John the Baptist, for example, reportedly called the Pharisees and the Sadducees a "generation of vipers."[33]

That's pretty strong language! As I stated earlier, Jesus reportedly denounced them for their self-righteousness, hypocrisy, and total focus on legal minutiae at the expense of people's needs. Interestingly, the Pharisees played a major role in Jesus' death. Both John the Baptist and Jesus of Nazareth were notable rabble-rousers whose following frightened the Jewish leadership. People in every age have a difficult time putting up with those who don't go along with the everyday, taken-for-granted beliefs and acts. Borg is right in pointing out that Jesus' vision of a compassionate God led him to live a compassionate life that crossed all the social boundaries and thereby threatened the existing socio-religious system. An adoption of his behaviors, which included mingling with all the impure, would have meant a total dissolution of Hebrew society because it would have called for a total rethinking of the purity system and all the social paraphernalia it had constructed over the centuries.

When our nation's young adults rebelled against the Viet Nam war and prevailing social and ethical norms in the 1960s the older adults in every city, town, and hamlet were beside themselves with rage and frustration. Few understood what had infected these young men and women. As I look back on that period I suspect the only thing that prevented masses of these young men

---

33 Matthew 3:7

and women from being rounded up and warehoused in prisons was the fact that everyone, in every social class, had a daughter or son who had signed on to what was called the *hippie peace movement*. Traditional moral and ethical bonds were thrown off and historic standards questioned. Woodstock and the shootings at Kent State University brought this new ethos into stark relief. It was a tough time for *so-called* Christian America.

As I explained earlier, while Jesus loved the law, he didn't appreciate what he believed to be its misinterpretation and abuse. Regardless of what you read in the New Testament regarding eating habits, there's little doubt Jesus followed the purity laws governing eating. While affirming the law as a moral blueprint for social and individual life, he emphasized that one should *focus on reflecting the grace, love, and compassion of God*. If one did that, obedience to the Law would take care of itself.

The Pharisees, and others, focused solely on an obedience that fulfills the letter of the law without understanding the meaning behind that law. They failed to understand God's concern for the total will of man. In other words, God not only forbids the actual acts of murder, stealing, and so forth, but—and this is important—the *person's inner will that leads to such acts as murder, abuse of another, and so forth*. Thus, Jesus' focus solely on compassion, as in a compassionate God, was a vision diametrically opposed to that held by the chief priests and scribes of that day.

You are probably wondering why we still keep making the Pharisee's mistake of focusing on the law. First, it's very seductive to do so. It's something a person can easily grasp, while loving an ornery neighbor—to say nothing of the unlovable—is wispy, wishy-washy, and hard to grasp. Second, it has to do with the fact that people in every age have a predisposition for *domesticating* sacred revelations.

By the way, people in our society who exhibit love and care for the down-and-outs, the enemy, and so forth, are loathingly labeled *bleeding heart liberals* by many. I've always found that strange, especially since it's generally hurled as a curse from people who sit in church every Sunday and pay homage to a man that epitomized radical love beyond human comprehension!

Besides, our sense of cultural civil justice prohibits us from throwing ourselves unabashedly into loving those we disagree with, who hurt our feelings, have broken the law, or are just plain unlovable! "By God," we cry, "that sucker oughta be horse whipped!" Or killed. For example, according to recent media polls a majority of Americans thought Houstonian Andrea Yates should have been sentenced to die for drowning her five children. "Pay the Piper," as the saying goes.

Americans worship law, any law. Just so it's a law. We can criminalize any behavior. Look cross-eyed at the wrong people and you'll end up in jail. Justice is our most important spiritual leader. A recent news release (August, 2002) reports that 6.6 million Americans are behind bars.[34] That's one out of every thirty-two people!

Given this history and cultural milieu, it should come as no surprise that our Christian institutions are composed of people whose main focus is on biblical law. True, many of the Hebrew laws—especially the Ten Commandments—are good moral guides. So much so that across America many community leaders fight to hang a copy of the Ten Commandments in schools and other public places. They do this under the mistaken belief that if people, especially children, will continually read these Commandments they will eventually appropriate those behaviors and clean up their act, so to speak. Who doesn't want everyone to do right? Who in their right mind can quarrel with Jesus' litany of evils of Mark 7:20, noted earlier? Everyone, regardless of their religious faith, should adhere to these behavioral principles. No argument from me. **However, adherence to these rules is not a requirement for receiving God's love and grace.**

But, and here's the thorn, history has shown that <u>knowing the law</u> and <u>obeying the law</u> are totally different things. Jesus knew of man's predisposition toward *anger, jealousy, hatred, insincerity,* and so forth. He was dead set against traditional legalisms and rituals that strive for external correctness while still harboring an impure will. This reveals the fact that God demands *the whole will of a person*

Jesus made this point by quoting Isaiah 29:13 as reported in Mark 7:6f and Matthew 15:8f:

> "These people honor me
>   with their lips,
> but their hearts are far from
>   me.
> They worship me in vain;
>   Their teachings are but rules
>   Taught by men."

---

34   <u>Houston Chronicle,</u> August 26, 2002, page 1.

There are times when Jesus is reportedly far more direct about this issue, as in Matthew 23:23 (see also the associated verses):

> "Woe to you, teachers of the law and Pharisees,
>   you hypocrites!
> You give a tenth of your spices—mint, dill and cumin,
>   But you have neglected the more important
>   matters of the law—justice, mercy and faithfulness."

Oh, oh! We're to have pure hearts and emphasize justice, mercy, and faithfulness. Are we in trouble here? I think so.

Most Americans would probably go along with the notion that we have the best criminal justice system in the world—such as it is. And no one would argue that it's perfect. It is always being refined. Nonetheless, how *just is it?* Are juries always and everywhere composed of one's peers? No. Are sentences always and everywhere equal? No. Do the rich and upper classes have an advantage? Yes. And so forth and so on. Justice within our society is relative, at best. And sometimes it just doesn't show up for work. A number of people convicted on murder charges have recently been released when newly established DNA blood tests determined their innocence. American justice is like the fickle finger of fate. And even the best of people err—whether pure of heart, honest, well meaning, or hard working. That's a reflection of the human condition. The nature of humankind.

But let's talk about divine justice. Does the One who created the universe and all that exists think in terms of justice, retribution, pay-back time, an eye-for-an-eye, getting even, settling grudges, balancing the scale, and so forth? One can certainly find a strain of that language throughout the Hebrew Bible to support that notion. But that's only one God concept. And Jesus didn't agree with it.

Jesus reportedly characterized God as compassionate and forgiving. For example, Jesus allegedly said:

> *You have heard that it was said, 'Love your neighbor and hate your enemy.' But I tell you: Love your enemies and pray for those who persecute you that you may be the sons of your Father in heaven. He causes sun to rise on the evil and the good, and sends rain on the righteous and the unrighteous.*[35]

---

[35] Matthew 5:43

And there are numerous stories that characterize a compassionate God as forgiving, caring, and non-judgmental—the story of the Prodigal Son, the owner of the vineyard, and many others.

Borg is right, by the way, when he points out that Christians often believe that the problem with the Law in Jesus' day was the establishment of a wrong set of rules.[36] All that's needed is a good set of Christian rules. But, as Paul writes, when this happens one is still living under the law.

> Christ is the end of the law.[37]

> It is for freedom that Christ has set us free.[38]

Philip Yancey adds further substance to our dilemma when he writes:[39]

> I grew up in a church that drew sharp lines between the age of law and the age of grace. While ignoring most moral prohibitions from the Old Testament, we had our own pecking order rivaling the Orthodox Jews'. At the top were smoking and drinking (this being the South, however, with its tobacco-dependent economy, some allowances were made for smoking). Movies ranked just below these vices, with many church members refusing even to attend *The Sound of Music*. Rock music, then in its infancy, was likewise regarded as an abomination, quite possibly demonic in origin.

> Other proscriptions—wearing makeup and jewelry, reading the Sunday paper, playing or watching sports on Sunday, mixed swimming (curiously termed "mixed bathing"), skirt length for girls, hair length for boys—were heeded or not heeded depending on a person's level of spirituality. I grew up with the strong impression that a person became spiritual by attending to these gray-area rules. For the life of me, I could not figure out much difference between the dispensations of Law and Grace.

> My visits to other churches have convinced me that this ladder-like approach to spirituality is nearly universal. Catholics, Mennonites, Churches of Christ, Lutherans, and Southern Baptists all have their own

---

36 Borg, Op. Cit., p. 105.
37 Romans 10:4
38 Galatians 5:1
39 Philip Yancey, <u>What's So Amazing About Grace?</u> (Grand Rapids, MI: Zondervan Press, 1997), p. 30.

custom agenda of legalism. You gain the church's, and presumably God's, approval by following the prescribed patterns.

Unfortunately, this pattern never seems to die. Now let's look at the difference between the Hebrew Bible and the Christian Bible to see if it helps us understand the *proper* role of the Law in our lives. Hopefully this discussion will shed light on our discussion about the nature of God.

Differences Between The Two Bibles

We've spent a lot of space discussing a general orientation to the Hebrew Bible. The following focuses on the Christian Bible so you can see how it differs from the Hebrew Bible. First, look at your Bible and notice that it's divided into two major parts: *Old* and *New*. Stop and think about that for a moment, since most Christians don't seem to do so.

The *old* means just that, *Old*. Now there's nothing wrong or disparaging about old. At least at my age I hope not. The *old* in relation to the *new* is the early Church's way of saying that the o*ld Covenant* relationship (via the Law) made between God and the Hebrews was replaced by a n*ew Covenant* that included *all humankind*—not just the Hebrews.

If we acknowledge that the event of Jesus the Christ established a *new covenant* that *replaced the old covenant* you can quickly see where this discussion is headed. In other words, humankind now lives in a totally *new relationship* with God. The Old relationship whereby people made God happy by obeying *the Law* has been replaced by a new relationship, one characterized through *justification by faith, through God's grace, or compassion*. The early apostolic fathers spoke of this latter path as the *fulfillment of the law,* which is what Paul refers to above.

Just so there's no misunderstanding, remember that Christianity claims that humans no longer live *under* the law of the Hebrew Bible, although the law is still there. As Paul states, "*Everything is permissible for me—but not everything is beneficial.*"[40] In other words, receiving God's love and acceptance is <u>not dependent</u> upon one's obeying any law.

Few people, if any, have been able to abide by the Old Testament law. And those that claim to have accomplished the feat become such self-righteous

---

40 I Corinthians 6:12, New International Version.

nincompoops that no one, including the historical Jesus, wanted much to do with them. Their life style plainly did not please God, at least according to Jesus of Nazareth. As you will discover, sooner than later I hope, few people appreciate people who claim to be—or acts as if—they are morally superior to others. Self-righteousness is an ugly sight.

Further, Christian tradition claims that the historical Jesus of Nazareth, while totally a man, was also fully God, meaning that He was the incarnation of God. *Wham!* That's a high-octane claim. In other words, a group of Hebrews in the first and second centuries issued the claim that in that historical *Jesus Event* the God who created and sustains all that exists had become flesh. They didn't stop at that declaration. They claimed that the incarnation was God's way of declaring *humankind* reconciled to Himself. That means God declared that he loves and accepts *everyone,* regardless of morality, wealth, education, race, nationality, language, or anything else. That love and acceptance means humankind is redeemed, no longer alienated from God. After the flood, so the story goes, God designated the rainbow as a sign of his covenant never to flood the earth again.[41] Speaking metaphorically, we can think of the incarnation, the God-Man MYSTERY, as the new sign from God that signifies His unequivocal love and compassion for humankind...

Further, the early disciples said that this Jesus event created a *new bond (covenant)* between God and people. There are no longer any *specially favored* people (read favored to mean those who obey the law). This new relationship with God extends to all people and is based solely on God's love and grace—not man's obedience to any law or other religiously imaginable activity. This is the *word about God*.

The claims that God became a human and that *somehow* this ACT constituted a universal reconciliation of man with God, and *solely by God*, is pretty strong stuff. Remember, this testimony of 2,000 years ago is not scientific. The written records about the events in Jesus' life are *faith interpretations* of what took place—through the use of mythology, via parables, simile, metaphors, and aphorisms. This is what the writers of the four Gospels mean when they refer to the eyes and ears of the heart.

In *seeing, hearing, and grasping the will* of this fundamental *kernel (Word from God)* the early believers worked hard to convey this view by symbolically

---

41   Genesis 9:12-13.

speaking and writing *about God*. All miracles, or wonder stories, etc., are vehicles meant to reveal the reality and essence of the God who revealed himself through this earthly incarnation. It is this *vitality*, or critical *Mysterious Word from God* that's hidden here, like a peach pit. It is here that God encounters us. (Read St. John 1:1.) Yet understanding this paradox has always been the Church's problem. *How can the mind of faith understand what the eye of faith sees?*

Unfortunately, people often get lost scurrying down some muddy road worrying about the grammar, or quarreling about the right interpretation, or trying to prove or disprove the scientific reality of biblical events, and fail to focus on this basic *kernel (the kerygma*, or *The Word in* the scriptures. This is the danger of focusing on man's word *about God*.

Some see a vast difference between the Hebrew and Christian Bibles. So much so that Albert Schweitzer, the great 19th Century missionary, reportedly refused to preach a sermon using the Hebrew Bible. In my opinion his position is not justifiable, although understandable. The OT is part of our Christian heritage, but it must be read and understood through the eyes of Christian tradition. I've constantly stressed the differences between the two works as a means of emphasizing their fundamental theological and historical divergence.

What Did Jesus Really Say? And Does It Matter?

People who have studied the scriptures seriously, which means keeping up with biblical scholarship, are keenly interested in how the Gospels reached their final form. We know, for example, that Jesus' original disciples passed on an oral tradition. This included what Jesus said and did, as well as what was said about him during those few years of his ministry.

This oral tradition period extends for *at least* two decades after Jesus' death. Remember, there were no printing presses and parchment (made from animal skins) and papyrus were expensive writing media. Besides, as hard as it is for us to believe, oral reports were more acceptable to people in those days. Furthermore, the best of minds in the best of times has a difficult time remembering precisely what the leader said. Therefore, not surprisingly, there were numerable variances.

The Jesus Seminar scholars recently concluded that some 80% of the words attributed to Jesus in the New Testament were not really spoken by Jesus. There are numerous layers of oral tradition that eventually show up piece-meal in fragments of written text. As the Jesus Seminar reports:[42]

> "…we do not have original copies of any of the gospels. We do not possess autographs of any of the books of the entire Bible. The oldest surviving copies of the gospels date from about one hundred and seventy-five years after the death of Jesus, and no two copies are precisely alike. And handmade manuscripts have almost always been 'corrected' here and there, often by more than one hand."

And, if scholars are correct, Jesus spoke Hebrew and Aramaic. But not Greek. And the only copies we have of the gospels are Greek. Thus, one should easily grasp the nature of our problem, if it is in fact a problem. In addition, there seems to have been a fairly large number of gospels being passed around. Twenty are known, but as Funk and Hoover report, the total number may have been higher.[43]

Let's make some sense out of what we have in the New Testament. Since Matthew, Mark, and Luke are so similar in views they have been called the *synoptic gospels*. And most scholars think Mark came into print first, around C.E. (common era) 70. Matthew and Luke followed some years later. Matthew and Luke supposedly borrowed from Mark and a few others, especially the Gospel of Thomas. But that's not all that you should know and understand. There are a number of Gospel parallels in print and it is easy to see how the Gospel contents line up.[44]

It should be noted up front that *writing style* is a critical distinction between the gospels. The Gospel of Mark is reportedly more colloquial, or akin to street language, whereas Luke wrote in a highly sophisticated Greek literary manner.[45]

On the other hand, it is easy to see that Matthew and Luke had much in common that was not in Mark. This suggests to scholars that they were probably using another document. This, by the way, has been known as the *Q Gospel*, which is now lost.[46] But they evidently had access to other written manuscripts.

---

42   Funk & Hoover, Op. Cit., p. 6.
43   Ibid., p. 29.
44   I would certainly recommend a careful reading of Funk & Hoover, the results of the Jesus Seminar group of scholars.
45   Ibid., p. xv.
46   Johannes Weiss, writing in German, referred to this document as Quelle (German for source). Thus, the Q document.

The Gospel of John showed up many years later and was clearly written for a Greek audience. Scholars are not sure how much he borrowed from the Synoptic and other sources. It certainly seems logical to assume that he was familiar with most, if not all, the existing documents and traditions.

Then there was the Gospel of Thomas, The Gospel of Philip, the Gospel of Peter, the Gospel of Truth, etc.[47] The Gospel of Thomas was found at modern day Bahnasa, located approximately 120 miles south of Cairo, Egypt.[48] It is a Coptic copy of an original Greek version that had been found in fragments at the turn of the 20th Century.[49] Thomas consists of a string of over one hundred sayings of Jesus, but no narrative regarding his life, death or resurrection.

The Gospel of Peter fragments relate the trial, death and resurrection of Jesus and scholars see it as dependent on Matthew et. al.[50] Two fragments were found. The earliest is a scroll fragment of a few verses dating from the second century C.E. The second, and larger fragment, found near Cairo, is of some sixty verses and is believed to date from the 600-900 C.E.[51]

The Gospel of Truth, according to Tannehill, "is an extended meditation on aspects of God and the world with scarcely any mention of Jesus explicitly (though with a number of possible allusions to traditions of Jesus' sayings).[52]

Interestingly, a comparison of the Q document and the Gospel of Thomas lead Crossan and Reed to state that the authors of both documents used common traditional sayings. There is no evidence suggesting either depended on the other for content.[53] Each writer did, however, use a significant amount of the traditional material in arguing his or her own specific theological case.

---

47 See a discussion by Robert C. Tannehill, "The Gospels and Narrative Literature," in The New Interpreter's Bible, Vol. VIII. (Nashville, Tn: Abingdon Press, 1995), p.56f. Other articles in the introduction to that volume are also excellent for synopsizing the problems we face with early writings, translations, and so forth. See also the excellent work by John Dominic Crossan & Jonathan L. Reed, Excavating Jesus:Beneath the Stones, Behind the Texts, (San Francisco: HarperCollins Publishers: 2001). P. 6f.
48 Crossan & Reed, Op. Cit., p. 9.
49 Ibid.
50 Ibid., p. 10.
51 Ibid.
52 Tannehill, Op. Cit., p. 72.
53 Crossan & Reed, Ibid.

There emerged in the second and third centuries a great deal of written material from which the Church selected the works framed into the Christian Bible; the New Testament. To some it is important to isolate what Jesus *really said and did* from what he was reported to have said and done. This focus is about *getting back to the historical Jesus* and was, to my knowledge, initiated by Hermann S. Reimarus (1694-1768), a professor in Hamburg, Germany. I first encountered the conversation by reading Albert Schweitzer's book, "The Quest of the Historical Jesus," back in the 1950s.

Bultmann, Barth and others who dominated the twentieth century theological world, believed it was impossible to discover the early layer of Jesus sayings, so it was passé to even pursue the issue. New scholars emerged in the 1980s and '90s to challenge this view.[54]

The task of isolating those elements that can be attributable to the historical Jesus is difficult and complicated, if not impossible. But for those to whom this quest is important it should be remembered that there were no printing presses. Manuscripts were copied by hand on sixteen-foot scrolls, or codices, and—most important—by those who had a passionate interest in the ministry of Jesus Christ. Therefore, the writers were prone to amend the former text to conform to their beliefs or to adapt it to counter whatever perceived threat to the Church they felt was at hand. Remember, they didn't have copyright laws or rules against plagiarism or amending of an original author's words.

Luke 2 relates the story of Mary and Joseph's trip from Nazareth to Bethlehem so Joseph could register for the census. Quirinius took a census in 10 B.C.E. and another in 6 C.E.[55] It's impossible to know which census Joseph and Mary attended. And it is historically inaccurate to claim that Herod the Great lived during Jesus's time.

Then Crossan and Reed, using archaeological data, use the case of Luke's story of Jesus' rejection in his home Synagogue at Nazareth to illustrate the problems the Church encounters in trying to correctly understand the historical Jesus.[56]

---

[54] A good discussion can be found in Funk & Hoover, Op. Cit., p. 2f.
[55] Fleming, James W., Transcription of Lectures of Women in the Bible, 1998., p. 25f.
[56] Crossan & Reed, Op. Cit, p. 27f.

In Luke 4:14-30, a young Jesus amazes the elders of the Synagogue with his profound wisdom. Then he makes his hearers mad. In fact, they got so mad they hauled him, presumably by force, to the "brow of the hill upon which the town was built, in order to throw him down the cliff."[57] All we are told is that he "walked through the crowd and went on his way."[58]

Or again, Crossan and Reed note that recent archaeology finds no Synagogue in Nazareth nor a high hill from which one can be thrown down. The authors believe that the author of Luke used his experiences in the larger cities and projected them upon the small hamlet of Nazareth (population between 200 to 400).[59] They summarize the argument by reporting:[60]

> Luke also presumes that a tiny hamlet like Nazareth had both a synagogue building and scrolls of scripture. The first presumption is most unlikely and…no evidence for a first-century synagogue building was discovered at Nazareth. The second presupposition is questionable—scrolls were mostly an urban privilege and, most likely, lectionary readings came later. A third presupposition, that there was some nearby cliff from which a miscreant could be hurled to his death, is simply false.
>
> …more important, Luke also assumes that Jesus is not only literate, but learned. He did not simply "began to teach" (Mark 6:2), he "stood to read" (6:4). Luke, himself a learned scholar, takes it utterly for granted, as do many modern scholars, that Jesus was literate and learned. This is very unlikely…The best specific work on ancient literacy in the Jewish homeland concludes about a 3 percent literacy rate…the prerogative of elite aristocrats…
>
> …That story is not only in, it is also from a later layer of the Jesus tradition. It is, in other words, an incident created by the evangelist Luke himself. It is, as presented, not history from Jesus' past in the Jewish homeland of the late 20s, but parable for Paul's future in the Jewish diaspora of the early 50s.

---

57   Luke 4:29.
58   Luke 4:30.
59   Crossan & Reed, Op. Cit., p. 30.
60   Ibid., p. 30-31.

Furthermore, Jim Fleming, a Biblical scholar who has spent many decades working as an archaeologist in Israel, claims that translators over the centuries were not averse to changing the gender endings when it suited their cultural predisposition. In an email Fleming says:

> "One of the main feminine endings that became masculine in the Middle Ages (1300 AD) was in Paul's greetings to the Romans in Chapter 16:7: 'Greet Adronicus, and Junia, my relatives who were in prison with me. They are prominent (noteworthy) among the apostles.' Junia is masculine, whereas Junias is feminine...Some religious leaders apparently gave her a sex change in the Middle Ages because they were convinced that no woman could be considered an apostle by St. Paul."[61]

Another illustration of editorial license driven by age-specific cultural reasons has to do with the feminine plurals

> "in the naming of children by the Patriarch and Matriarch narratives in Genesis (Genesis 25:25, 'so they named him Esau.' The *they* in Hebrew is a feminine plural and Matriarchs and midwives named children in this period. One cannot tell the English *they* is masculine or feminine. But in the Middle Ages *they* was a masculine plural because the religious leaders believed that only men had authority to name children.[62]

Unfortunately, many don't want to hear this type information. Somehow it seems to threaten them. Nonsense. Remember, *the Truth* is in the Christ who encounters one through the Scriptures. What Mark was trying to communicate is still intact. The Spirit of God transcends any spoken or written letters, as I've constantly stressed. Crossan and Reed continue by saying:[63]

> All of that serves to vindicate the importance of layering analysis not just in an archaeological mound, but also in a gospel text. **Luke is not telling a lie and does not intentionally defame the people of Nazareth. He retrojects the serious and even lethal opposition to Paul in the later Jewish diaspora onto the earliest experience of Jesus in the Jewish homeland.** (Emphasis mine.)

---

61 Fleming, Jim, Correspondance, April 7, 2004.
62 Ibid.
63 Ibid.

Don E. Post, Ph.D.

Reflections on the Quest for the Real Historical Jesus

Briefly, the Enlightenment, in addition to changing our fundamental worldview from an objective to subjective one, claimed to discover Christian truth through historical means. The Church's historical dogma and creeds were out. The *ultimate truth* would be found by identifying the historical Jesus through a rigorous historical analysis.

This quest, it seems to me, as intriguing as it may be, solved very little. The Event is comprised as much by what witnesses claim he said and did as it is with what he literally said and did. The fundamental testimony was, and still is, that in a human being named Jesus, the God of history reconciled the world. And the fundamental issue was, and still is, "Who do you say I am?" This was Jesus' challenging question to Peter in Matthew 16:13. No image of the historical Jesus can change this challenge. Therefore, as much as I enjoy the work of the Jesus Seminar, I find myself in the aftermath asking, "So what does it matter if Jesus said or didn't say this or that?"

Meanwhile, our historical skepticism is fed by the *subjectivism* loosed during the Enlightenment. Prior to that time a notion of objective reality characterized the worldview of our European ancestors. Now, however, man has become the measure of all things. Whereas the traditional worldview believed that God manifested Himself in an objective act or in true doctrine (creeds), all of which were certified by the Church or the Bible, now we view revelation as a subjective affair. Church authority and creeds are now highly suspect.

Our modern worldview is, henceforth, dominated by radical individualism and we have become *narcissists* (people who excessively admire themselves). Everyone becomes his or her own authority. So we end up creating a Jesus after our own image. This can be seen in our love of Sallman's *Head of Christ* that hangs in most American churches and in the numerous novels and films presuming to represent the historical Jesus. These are too numerous to list, by the way.

Hence, we define Jesus' relevance in individualistic terms. To most modern Christians Jesus is viewed as the *perfect example* of what it means to be human. Interestingly, our remodeling of Jesus always turns out to be a reflection of the psychological and social theories that dominate our times.

All these changes do not paint a pretty picture of the Church. The loss of Christian history and the demonization of the historic creeds suggest to me that we've *thrown the baby out with the wash*. We didn't need to do that and we are the weaker for it.

The preceding provides a glimpse of some key historical differences between the Hebrew Bible and the Christian Bibles and the importance of both. In my next letter I'll discuss how the Christian Bible came into existence.

FOURTH LETTER

Shaa-zam & Presto! The Christian Bible

Dear Ben and Grace,

Given the background so far, I'm sure you are wondering how the particular books and letters that comprise the New Testament were *canonized*, or selected to be in the Bible. Canon is a Greek word, kavwn, or kannon, meaning root, reed, measuring rod, rule, and so forth. Its origin is in ancient Sumaria.[64] Canon was applied metaphorically[65] to denote the norms by which everything in the church should be measured.

The Old Testament used by early Christians was a Greek version known as the Septuagint; scholars refer to this as LXX, after the 70 translators who reputedly worked on it during the time of Ptolemy Philadelphus, 285-246 B.C.E.[66] The oldest copies of the LXX used dates from the 4th century and were copied many times by Christian hands. It should also be noted that these early copiers were not subject to our contemporary rules of writing. They were not averse to changing the text to conform to prevailing ideas and values.

---

64 See Joseph Henry Thayer (ed), Op. Cit.
65 Webster defines a metaphor as an application of a word or phrase to an object or concept, which it does not literally denote, in order to suggest a comparison. Example: The world is a stage.
66 Henry Snyder Gehman (ed.) The New Westminster Dictionary of the Bible, (Philadelpia: The Westminster Press, 1970), p. 971.

Greek Manuscript, fr. Egypt, 2nd Century C.E.[67]

However, the Hebrew canon was probably not fixed at Jesus's time. The first to identify an acceptable collection of documents was the Jewish historian Flavius Josephus. (born 37 C.E.—died approximately 100 C.E.).[68] On the one hand he states that the canon was closed at the time of Ezra. But today Protestants, Catholics, and Eastern Orthodox branches differ about which books belong in the Old Testament. Josephus's Old Testament canon did not include Ecclesiastes, a book that everyone, Jewish and Christian, now accept.

First, be aware that there is *good* biblical scholarship and *bad* biblical scholarship. Good scholarship is the pursuit of truth for the sake of truth, no matter where the investigation leads. *Bad* biblical scholarship, on the other hand, results from a predetermined truth where the analyst is only trying to cloak his belief in scientific garb. The latter's search is just a façade. And, unfortunately, it seems that *good* scholarship, honest truth seeking, is impossible for people of a fundamentalist persuasion who operate out of a theological mind-set that claims absolute infallibility of the words in the Bible. Any finding that threatens that position is instantaneously dismissed. You should beware of such snake oil salesmen parading in Christian garb.

In regard to the truth, the scholars of the Jesus Seminar ask,

> If the spirit dictated gospels that are inerrant, or at least inspired, why is it that those who hold this view are unable to agree on the picture of Jesus found in those same gospels?…The endless proliferation of views of Jesus on the part of those who claim infallibility for the documents erodes confidence in that theological point of view and in the devotion to the Bible it supports.[69]

Another question that punctures the inerrancy of the Scriptures is, "Why, if God took such pains to preserve an inerrant text for posterity, did the spirit not provide for the preservation of original or autographed copies of the gospels?"[70]

---

67 In the public domain.
68 Josephus, Flavius, Jewish Antiquities. (Ca. 100 C.E.)
69 Funk & Hoover, Op.Cit., p. 5f.
70 Ibid., p. 6.

Good questions. However, it seems to me that the heart of the first century testimony, the *kerygma* (divine activity), is plainly, and unequivocally there. The *paradoxical compound* found throughout the four Gospels claims that *Jesus was fully human and fully God*. This compound formula is quite clearly stated throughout the New Testament. Further, it also seems clear that this is a MYSTERY of God about which we can say nothing literal. To do so is to domesticate the God-Man MYSTERY. And all our language about this MYSTERY, whether we focus on the act of creation, incarnation, or salvation, is finally beyond the capability of human speech, as I noted in an earlier letter.

In the first century of the Christian era, the Hebrew Bible was the only Holy Book available to the followers of Jesus Christ. Again, don't forget that the early disciples of Jesus Christ comprised a *sect* within the Jewish community. The Hebrew Bible was their Bible. They were Jews. They didn't set out to write another set of Scriptures.

The stories and sayings of Jesus' life, death, and resurrection floated around as oral tradition for decades after his death. The Gospel of Matthew (90 C.E.) has always been the most popular report of Jesus' life and was clearly written to a Jewish community.[71] Some, most notably my old Professor Albert Outler,[72] are convinced that Matthew was written first. Others disagree.

The book of Mark (70 C.E.) seems to have been written for a Gentile community no longer living under the Judean Torah.[73] Tradition reports that a physician who was one of Paul's companions wrote Luke, but we don't know for sure. As stated previously, the earliest manuscripts we have are from the second or third century, around 175-225 C.E.[74]

John is the Fourth Gospel and latecomer. The matter of authorship is further mystified by the fact that the manuscript did not show up until the early years

---

71 M. Eugene Boring, "The Gospel of Matthew," in <u>The New Interpreter's Bible</u>, Vol. VIII, (Nashville, TN:Abingdon Press, 1995), p. 94. You should be aware, however, that my old Seminary professor, Dr. Albert Outler, now deceased, didn't agree. He believed that Matthew was probably first. See Albert Cook Outler (Thomas Oden, ed), <u>Christology,</u> Vol 4, (Anderson, Indiana:Bristol House, 1996), p. 26f.
72 Albert Cook Outler (Thomas Oden, ed), <u>Christology,</u> Vol 4, (Anderson, Indiana:Bristol House, 1996), p. 26f.
73 <u>Ibid</u>., p. 95.
74 R. Alan Culpepper, "The Gospel of Luke," in <u>The New Interpreter's Bible,</u> Vol. IX, (Nashville, TN: Abingdon Press, 1995), p. 4.

of the second century CE. If the author was, in fact, John the son of Zebedee, as some presume, then he either lived over a hundred years or the manuscript was hidden all those years.

Scholars also tell us that once the documents started to circulate they were usually bundled together. The four Gospels (Matthew, Mark, Luke, John) were packaged together, and the letters of Paul came as a unit. The Book of Acts could be attached to either package.

The sole purpose of writing the Gospels was to relate the **MYSTERIOUS** story of Jesus to a number of different publics. One of the most persuasive arguments for Matthew as the first written is the fact that it is the most Jewish of the lot. That is, as a Jewish group the early disciples would naturally relate the story with a Jewish perspective. If not written first it was obviously placed first in any and all Gospel compilations. But who wrote what and when, as interesting as that may be, really doesn't matter.

Nevertheless, the historic process that led to their writing and the problems inherent in transcribing these documents by hand through the centuries deposits a lot of problems at our door. Many hands were involved. It is difficult to copy anything precisely, regardless of the technology! Very difficult. The early copiers experienced errors in copying anything of great length, just as we do today. And, by the way, as I noted earlier, a copier would often edit the text to fit his own thoughts, the prevailing theological winds, or to correlate with what he had been told via the oral tradition. It was not unethical to do this.

For example, most scholars deny the Apostle Paul's authorship of 1st and 2nd Timothy and Titus, which view women as subordinate to men in society and the church. The author is generally thought to be someone in the second or third century who sought to edit Paul's views so they would conform to prevailing ideas about women. But you must also remember that the Pastoral letters (those written to the early churches advising proper beliefs and behavior) were never viewed as equal to the four Gospels.

Ultimately the existing writings held up through common usage and agreement from the Councils of Nicea (325 C.E.) and Constantinople (381 C.E.). Although the main body of literature was in common usage by the end of the second century, it *was not until the fourth century that the dust had finally settled and the Testaments were agreed upon.* They were decreed as the official documents of the Church (canonized). These documents, therefore, became the accepted *riverbed* of Church belief. Any area outside that riverbed was, and still is, heresy land. *Heresy*, by the way, is any interpretation of the Christian message that weakens it or renders the evangelistic message useless.

Professor Outler correctly understood the *Christocentric focus* of the letters that were canonized. He provided us a unique answer for why the canonizers only chose four Gospels and not five, six or whatever. He cites St. Irenaeus as explaining that "there are four winds, only four points on the compass, only four corners of the earth—hence, only four Gospels."[75] That makes sense. It reflects the first century three-story, flat earth worldview.

Further, to Professor Outler the order in which the Gospels and letters were organized was no mystery. First, there is a Christocentric focus to all the NT writings. Second, it was impossible to contain in one document the many facts of the God-Man Jesus.[76] And since the first challenge the Jewish disciples of Jesus faced was to convince their fellow Jews of Jesus' Messiahship, it was only logical that they put the Gospel of Matthew first. It was, after all, written for that very purpose.

Outler viewed the Markan image of Jesus as more action-minded than message-minded. It is, therefore, more appropriate reading for the disciples of Peter in Rome.[77] Mark's emphasis on the passion and the resurrection is clearly pertinent to the early Christian martyrs of Rome.

But, continues Outler, the early Church also had to sell Jesus to Greeks who lacked an understanding of Judaism. To this end Outler sees Luke as the "connected narrative" directed at the Greeks.[78] Furthermore, it is logical for the writer of Luke to follow up his Gospel narrative with a sequel, which is the Book of Acts. The Gospel of John split the writer of the Lukan works (Gospel and Acts) apart to insert a more cosmic perspective, which essentially means it adopted Greek (Hellenistic) concepts and worldviews.

The original issue was determining how many facets of the God-man Jesus should be covered? Outler states that he would have voted for five, adding the Book of Hebrews, where the God-man is conceptualized as our Great High

---

75 Outler, Op. Cit., p. 27.
76 Ibid., p. 26.
77 Ibid, p. 27.
78 Ibid.

Priest. Outler's historic early Catholic interests are transparent in this idea. But, he rightly argues that the paradox of the God-man theme runs consistently through Matthew, Mark, Luke, John, and then Hebrews. The Book of Acts is an effective bridge between the four Gospels and Paul's interpretative, theological writings.

The *Pastoral letters* provide a sketch of the early Church's life and ministry. The Book of Hebrews may have been used as the bookend, as Outler suggests, or as a way of balancing the message of the *Christ of faith* and the *Jesus of history*.

The NT canon begins with the terms and order of our salvation in Christ and moves to the meaning of human existence as expressed in the Pauline writings. Of the Pauline writings, Romans was inserted first because it is the "most complete summary of the Pauline message."[79]

At this point in his sketch of the canonization process, Outler provides an interesting scenario. He states:

> "...the Pauline message has a tendency to discount the narrative stories of the Gospels in favor of a more heavily theological comment. The canon makers saw a difficulty here, so they added Hebrews to the cluster as if it were Paul's own. In this, they thought to redress the balance in the New Testament between the Christ of faith and the Jesus of history."[80]

He then adds:

> "The Pastorals take us a generation further into the life and work of the early church as an institution (it had not appeared as one in any of the Gospels, Acts, or the Pauline letters). The General Epistles give us a glimpse of the spread and diversity of non-Pauline Christianity—Jacobite, Petrine, and Johannine. And because it would never have done to conclude the canon with Jude, the Apocalypse rounds it off—not with a whimper but a bang!"[81]

Summarily, *we don't know who wrote any of the New Testament books and letters. We only have some educated guesses.*

---

79   Ibid.
80   Ibid.
81   Ibid.

Don E. Post, Ph.D.

Marcion and the Great Discontinuity Between the Bibles

As the debate about Jesus Christ within the synagogues intensified in those first few centuries, it became clear to the Greeks that something was amiss in the Hebrew Scriptures. The debate involved not only the meaning of Jesus but the Hebrew Scriptures themselves. Jesus' revelation of God as pure compassionate love and grace didn't coincide with the angry, jealous, and vindictive God so dominant in the OT. One of the key proponents of this position was a man called Marcion, who lived in the first half of the second century.

Raised in a seaport on the south coast of the Black Sea and the son of a bishop, Marcion found his way to Rome and attached himself to the local Christian group. He felt Paul understood the sharp distinction between the OT law and the compassionate grace of Christ found in the New Testament.

Briefly, Marcion declared that the early Christian Church had polluted the Gospel of Jesus Christ by trying to blend it with Judaism. He maintained that the God of the OT was an evil creature and not the one talked about by Jesus of Nazareth. He argued that this Old Testament God was an evil creature, which he labeled the *demiurge* after the fashion of the Platonists, is responsible for all the evil in the world.[82] On the other hand, the God of Jesus Christ had been hidden until revealing himself in and through Jesus Christ. And this newly revealed God was pure, unbounded grace and love. This is the God Paul talked about who loves humankind in spite of human's lack of merit. Thus, as the biblical scholar Justo L. Gonzalez says, "Marcion and Judaism agree that there is *no continuity* between the Hebrew Scriptures and what Christians proclaim."[83]

Marcion's view found opposition. Tertullian, a key leader in the early church, and others, took Marcion to task by asking where this loving creature had been hiding over the centuries while the evil *demigurge* was creating havoc in the world. Marcion's views weren't widely accepted, and he was finally cut off from the Church. Gonzalez sums up the opposing line of thought well:

---

82 See the discussion in: Kenneth Scott Latourette, A History of Christianity, (New York: Harper & Brothers, 1953), p. 125f; and, Justo L. Gonzalez, "How the Bible Has Been Interpreted in Christian Tradition," in The New Interpreter's Bible, (Nashville: Abingdon Press, 1994), p. 84f.
83 Gonzalez, Op. Cit., p. 85.

> To deny all validity to the OT is to turn Christianity into a religion that has nothing to do with human history and to make its God a Johnny-come-lately whose supposed love for humanity is thereby implicitly denied.... It denied the doctrine of creation and, by implication, of providence. By making the physical world evil, it tended to imply that the Savior could not have come in the flesh...[84]

The Christian Bible is basically the early Church's work of interpreting the Hebrew Bible in the light of the Jesus God-Man MYSTERY. The early Church fathers strongly believed that the Hebrew Scriptures were, in fact, Christian Scripture *if interpreted through the eyes of Christian faith.*

A number of controversies consumed early church leaders, but the Marcion issue is a key one and provides a flavor of the debates that plagued the early church.

Ways of Interpreting Scripture

But how should one, in any age, interpret Scripture? This has always been a huge and painful cockle-burr under the saddle of Christians. In some periods it has been a bigger problem than in others. For example, today there is little argument that one's understanding of a biblical book begins by understanding the historical context in which the author was writing. We ask about a text's original intent within a particular historical context. Then we ask if it has meaning for our time, if at all.

Not so the early Christians. They assumed the Hebrew Scriptures had meaning for them in their time and looked for that meaning. They interpreted ancient texts as prophecy, allegory, typology, or a combination of these.

Reading Scripture as **prophecy** seems to have been the preferred choice within the early Church. Matthew, for example, consistently views OT texts as prophecy. The writer sees the birth of Jesus as a fulfillment of OT prophecy, saying in Isaiah 1:22 (NIV), "All this took place to fulfill what the Lord had said through the prophet."

---

[84] *Ibid*. Gonzalez has a fine discussion of various historical modes of interpreting Scripture.

Contrast this with Isaiah 7:14 (NIV) where it is written: "Therefore the Lord himself will give you a sign: The virgin will be with child and will give birth to a son, and will call him Immanuel." Numerous God-Man **mysteries** are reported in Matthew to fulfill prophecies found in the Hebrew Bible: Jesus' Bethlehem birth, the slaughter of innocents, and so forth.

Nevertheless, scholars have long noted the problems inherent in viewing Scripture solely as prophecy. Numerous texts were developed in the early church that purportedly demonstrated the prophetic nature of Scripture. This means that the text, or texts, had nothing to do with current people and times but was for some unforeseen future. Gonzalez finds two main problems with the contemporary practice of viewing Revelations as a futuristic piece.[85]

First, if one were to start with Genesis 1:1 and go through the whole OT marking those texts that seem to be prophetic, most of the material would be unmarked. Gonzalez states:

> Do we simply declare that, because they do not foretell the future, they are not part of God's revelation? Do we simply ignore them, declaring that they are no longer relevant? The reading of the OT as prophecy, although applicable to some passages, is useless for most others.[86]

The second problem with reading the Bible through the lens of prophecy is that it limits a text's applicability and ultimate authority on whether or not the God-Man **Mystery** is fulfilled. What possible meaning could Scripture have for intervening generations? None. And to read Revelations through the eyes of prophecy is to miss the meaning it had for those early century Christian Jews who saw Rome as beast and tyrant. The book *is not some magical futurist blueprint.*

The next method of interpreting biblical text was through **allegory**, which means that spiritual or abstract ideas are interpreted in concrete forms. The allegorical interpretation of ancient myths had a long history among these early people, especially the Greeks. But the biblical scrolls found at *Qumran* also share this method of interpretation.

Among the early Church fathers, Origen, a famous teacher in Alexandria during the early third century, strongly pushed the allegorical method in

---

85 Ibid., p. 87.
86 Ibid., p. 88.

interpreting Scripture. He contended that Scripture has three meanings: a literal, or historical meaning, a moral or psychic meaning, and a spiritual or intellectual meaning.[87] He reportedly approached every text looking for hidden, or allegorical, meaning.

Origin has been criticized for making the Bible a huge puzzle and leaving the impression that he had all the keys to the proper interpretation. Further, Origin believed that Scripture must be interpreted within the community of faith because it is subject to what he called *the rule of faith*. That is, *the Scriptures were written by the hands of faith and only have meaning through the eyes of faith.*

Allegorical interpretation has a decided advantage over prophecy, since every verse is allegorically important. And, allegory sees Scripture as tied to eternal and moral truths and not to the historical God-Man MYSTERY.

On the other hand, **typology**, the third historical means of interpreting Scripture finds meaning in the historical God-Man MYSTERY itself and not in allegory or prophecy. Early church fathers such as Justin Martyr and Irenaeus, bishop of Lyons, found the typological method of interpreting Scripture the most meaningful. Typology goes beyond prophecy by seeing God-Man MYSTERIES as pointing to other God-Man MYSTERIES.

Justin Martyr[88]

Typology can get somewhat weird, as when Paul uses it to say (I Cor. 10:4 NIV), "for they drank from the spiritual rock that accompanied them, and that rock was Christ."

To this day we are not agreed upon how to interpret Scripture. One can hear every conceivable mode preached from pulpits throughout Christendom on a weekly basis. Some preachers make up new ones as they go along. The Biblical God-Man MYSTERY is generally presented metaphorically.

Outler reminds us that,

> ...there is a profound difference between the authority of the New Testament witness to the actuality of God's Mystery in Jesus Christ and

---

87   Ibid., p. 89.
88   In the public domain.

the authority of the New Testament interpretations of that Mystery. The latter may quite legitimately be interpreted and developed, as indeed they have been, in almost every age.[89]

Thus, to confuse the *Word of God* with the *words of the witnesses* to the Word of God is to confuse the whole God-Man MYSTERY. The purpose of the Scriptures is to reveal the *Mysterious God-in-Christ* and not to give us some scientific formula by which we can harness God's power or domesticate Him in some fashion. *If* the Jesus God-Man MYSTERY is the Christ God-Man MYSTERY, and I believe it is, then it cannot be interpreted by our keenest or most brilliant verbal concoctions.

Always remember, God never asks a person, at any time or in any place, to sacrifice the mind in order to be a faithful companion. You will meet people who wear their lack of knowledge as a badge of honor, saying, "Oh, no, if the Bible says Jonah was eaten by a large fish and after three days and nights was vomited up on shore, then I believe it happened just that way."[90]

Give me a break! When pushed to defend the God-Man MYSTERY as an accurate historical account, knowing what is known about big fish, the digestive process, and Jesus's revelation of God, such a fundy will retort, "Don't you believe God can do whatever he wants to do?"

If you agree that God can do whatever he wants to do, the literalist ends the discussion with, "Thar ya go. Case closed." Hogwash. But, while our common intelligence suggests that such biblical God-Man MYSTERIES are not to be taken literally, they are *to be taken seriously.*

Or again, to interpret Genesis 3:8, when God reportedly "was walking in the cool of the day," as meaning that God literally walked in a garden is to take leave of one's senses. *But, the metaphor is to be taken very seriously by people of faith.*

Unfortunately, this brief sketch does not do justice to the decades of arguing, fussing, quarreling, and down right meanness that has taken place among competing groups as each sought to exert their will on the interpretation of the Bible. Hopefully you will take time to read a good history of Christianity and grasp this process. Also, you will see that nothing much has changed over the

---

89   Ibid., p. 43.
90   Jonah 1:17f.

centuries, church people still argue, fuss, quarrel, and get downright mean and hateful over all kinds of issues! This has never been a sterling witness for the Church, but…it's what happens when Jesus's followers try to **domesticate** the God-Man Jesus.

Now that I've oriented you to the biblical materials, it's time to discuss human nature. Little of the preceding makes much sense if one doesn't have a good grasp of human nature. You will hear people account for all kinds of acts as stemming from that amorphous thing called *human nature*. Humans can do be grisly evil creatures on the one hand and such loving, selfless beings on the other. We do seem to be an enigmatic creature.

FIFTH LETTER

BEAUTY AND THE BEAST

Dear Ben and Grace,

Now that you've an introduction to the biblical dramas and the problems associated with interpreting scripture, we can move on to the thorny issue of human nature and the meaning of human existence. I guess this letter could be called a discussion of the *long-legged beasties*.[91] Our dualistic nature of good and evil has long been recognized.

All orally transmitted myths and the majority of literature, regardless of origin, view human nature as a creation of the gods, or a god. The relation between humans and their creator(s) is almost always characterized by conflict and man's attempts to placate the god or gods. The Bible uses numerous literary devices to explain this conflict as a battle between God's will and ours. In this letter I'll set forth some key universal issues against the backdrop of contemporary Western thinking. Briefly, our 21st Century Christian self-understanding results from changes in technology, the rise of a democratic individualism (rights of the individual), historic fears associated with death, and the universal forces of nature, to name a few of the most notorious reasons.

---

91 Two face sketch by Tony Karpm used by permission. See Techno-Impressionist Museum at www.techno-impressionist.com.

Don E. Post, Ph.D.

Western Identity Problems

I'll start by discussing a familiar psychological view of our predicament. Americans are totally committed to individualism. Personal identity is unarguably our most cherished social possession. The question is variously raised as, "Who am I?" Or, "What is life all about?" Westerners in general, and Americans specifically, are neurotically fixated on the self. We are the world's supreme navel gazers.

By contrast, traditional, non-Western cultures don't have our identity problems. Children are taught that they are members of a particular family, clan, or tribe. And there are no other choices. Period. No discussion. Little or no deviation is allowed. A person's identity is that of the group and Western individualism does not exist. One's choices are highly constricted, even marriage.

In traditional, non-Western societies there is little tolerance for fudging, or deviancy. That's still true in the majority of non-Western societies. There are deviants in every society, of course and they are dealt with swiftly and harshly. Children exploring the outer boundaries of rules are immediately punished. Finally, when one reaches adulthood and still hasn't got the message he/she can be banished from the group. Banishment is a devastating act, because one's identity is totally wrapped up in the group and all physical and social support mechanisms are removed. It's tantamount to death! Those cultures occupying very marginal environments, such as the Inuit of the Polar regions, have traditionally provided relatively narrow limits for member choices. You got along or were dumped to make it on your own in the harsh climate and there was no way an individual could survive alone.

It seems to me no accident that psychiatry developed in the industrial West. Industrialization technology, for whatever else it did, spawned cities and individualism, which had disastrous consequences for traditional social patterns. Kinship and other social cohesive mechanisms of traditional relations suffered irreparable alterations. People felt lost, or disengaged from the social nets holding their lives together. They felt uprooted. All the constraint devices and associated social supports were so weak as to be useless or they were completely gone.

Contrastively, a contemporary Westerner has to mull over a jillion issues without the help of a traditional clan, tribe, or extended family. The loss of traditional social controls, with their enormous security support, has led to a radical increase in psychological dysfunctions ala increased crime rates, the destruction of the traditional family, and so forth and so on.

To place all responsibilities for coping with life totally upon an individual is an enormous load. Many people can't cope in an urban environment. Americans worry and fret about numerous decisions on a daily basis. What should I do for a living? What should I wear? Whom should I marry? Should I be seen with this or that person? What will people think if I do this…or that? On and on it goes. We are always watching the reactions of others around us for clues as to proper behavior. We are never sure of the rules because they change from group to group. Lacking traditional social supports most people grasp peer group ethics and discipline, which leaves our society fractured.

Westerners want desperately to be accepted by others primarily because we feel so uncomfortably estranged, lost, and/or unnoticed. The lengths we will go to be accepted and noticed are incredible! We'll mutilate our bodies, abuse those our social clique sees as weaker, uglier, dumber, fatter, skinnier, taller, shorter, or speak a different language, follow a different religion, or believe differently. We can even go so far as to assist in killing those who are different from our own social reference group—as far-fetched as that may have seemed a few short years ago. Random drive-by killings and abusive behavior of others have become daily fare in America.

Adapting to social groups, or being socialized, is part of the human experience. Over the years as a college professor, I watched entering freshmen wander on to campus dressed in the fashionable garb of their hometown high school, speaking their hometown's colloquial language, and holding on to hometown values. By the end of the first semester, they were transformed. They took on the prevailing dress norms of the college campus crowd, dropped most of their linguistic dialects, and speech patterns were altered.

Families who migrate from one region of the States to another experience this same social transformation. Local patterns of behavior and thought gradually replace former patterns, usually unconsciously.

Non-Westerners don't experience the problem of self-identity to the degree we do because they're not cut off from their historic socio-cultural roots. Not yet. But traditional peoples around the world are becoming more aware of Western cultural threats to their worldviews and patterns of life. As an example, this is a major reason traditional Arab Muslims, for example, look upon Western cultures as evil. The attack on the World Trade Center in September 2001, was a military tactic carried out by a group within Islam who view the West as an evil threat to their way of life and existence.

As the most basic level of life, one's personal identity is always a social identity issue, whether born into a simple traditional or complex modern society. Sociologists speak of newborn babies as *infant barbarian invaders*.[92] This may sound crude, but it's an appropriate expression because newborns have to learn what it means to be a human being.

The process of learning to be a human is called the *socialization process*. Infants, as a mass of protoplasm, only have the biological equipment for learning. They are not endowed with human attributes. Unfortunately! Any parent can testify to the wrenching metamorphous wherein an infant barbarian invader becomes a socially acceptable human being. Social scientists claim that *every human is a social construction dependent upon his or her social nurturing group for self-meaning*.

So, given that (1) every person born into this world faces the primary task of self-discovery, and (2) that self-identification is a social process, and, (3) that Westerners have, for the most part, been disconnected from their social past, it follows that we have special problems with self-identity, social estrangement, and meaninglessness. This is not an enviable predicament. In spite of the fact that Westerners have developed amazing technological advances, hundreds of thousands have fallen through the crack because they weren't able to adjust and cope with social complexity. This is revealed in our Western increasing rates of suicide, addictions, mental illness, and a host of other societal ills that simpler traditional societies generally escape. This doesn't mean that people in non-Western traditional societies don't have their problems. They do. But not these.

Things That Go Bump In the Night!

In addition to the preceding problems associated with our understanding of being human, we have always, in all times and places, had a keen sense of finiteness and the awesome power of natural forces. First, death has always been a frightening phenomenon. To see a loved one die and find that the personality no longer exists in the *here-and-now* has been a great puzzle, at least as far back

---

[92] Courtesy of Dr. O.Z. White, retired Professor of Sociology, Trinity University, San Antonio, Texas. Now retired.

as the Neanderthaloids.[93] Numerous tools and personal possessions have been found in Neanderthal graves, indicating the belief that the person was passing to another world. Since that time all people have held beliefs about life after death.

Humankind has also wrestled with understanding the forces of nature. Children are generally frightened by lightning and thunder. Adults should be, if they have a modicum of common sense. This fear is gradually coupled with the uncontrollable forces of tornadoes, floods, fires, diseases, and other such. Until lately few understood the science behind such natural phenomena. I've been caught in some hair-raising earthquakes in Asia and found them to be pretty scary experiences. But I understood earthquakes through science, not metaphysics.

But pre-scientific people saw a huge hand behind nature's behavior. They were convinced that *someone was out there*. Although science has overcome the superstitious myths about lightning, thunder, floods, tornados, earthquakes and such, it is not difficult to understand how easily people can attach a personality to natural phenomena.

This world is an amazing creation. The more we learn about the expanse of the universe, the more awesome it becomes. As one looks out upon this universe, with all its mystery, power, complexity, and beauty, it is impossible not to ask, "How did this come to be?" Scratch the skin of any thoughtful agnostic and you'll find some notion about a larger metaphysical being.

This sense of the sacred attached to Mother Nature manifests itself in human thought in at least two ways. First, a people believe that God causes acts of nature, or second, such events result from the laws of nature and people get in the way from time to time. True, you will often find a person who views creation as an accident. Most, however, still agree with our pre-scientific ancestors that there is some kind of discrete being that feels, thinks, and acts, who is *out there or around here*, for good and evil. In other words, they see a rational force behind creation. All creation mythologies, wherever found, explain creation and acts of nature as the result of a metaphysical god or gods. Most people sense a sacred aspect to life to some degree.

---

93 Most physical anthropologists classify the various Neanderthals as an early subspecies of Homo sapiens. They are referred to as a subspecies of our own species because the size of their brain. Cranial capacities range from 1300 to 1600 cc, which means some of them had bigger brains than we do. The Neanderthals date back as far as 200,000 years ago. They persisted in time and were gradually replaced by Homo sapiens sapiens.

So, traditional people have historically believed that their God actively manipulates natural phenomena. So, if a person is hit and killed by a bolt of lightening it was a direct and intentional act of God. The same view applies to floods, earthquakes, or any other damaging natural act. God did it. Many contemporary people seem to share this view.

It's interesting to hear from 21st Century people who escape a flood, fire, tornado, or other natural act. I'm amazed at how they thank God for being spared. They imply that God was directly responsible for the act, and, for some unknown reason, chose to spare them while killing others. Insurance policies even refer to natural phenomena as acts of God. A recent CBS program (60 Minutes) had a female TV evangelist who said that God was directly responsible for every single act in life.

The scientific worldview, on the other hand, sees Mother Nature's acts as the result of natural law and account for such acts as random. In the scientific worldview God does not interfere in the normal activity of Mother Nature. So we have a contrast between an active God and a passive God in relation to Mother Nature.

Summarily, a shallow social-net and competing definitions of *right behavior* hamper our Western search for identity and meaning in life. In culturally pluralistic America few of us agree on the rightness of anything. We are urged to narcissism. "Do their own thing," has become a popular expression in America. Traditional values and norms are viewed as out of date. This *Enlightenment legacy* means that you've got a greater dilemma to work through than our non-Western cousins. How thrilling.

So much for the secular approach to human nature. The Christian view of human nature is rooted in early Hebrew lore. The creation stories (plural) found in the Book of Genesis attempt to account for human nature and the issues of good and evil.

The Hebrew Legends of the Creation and the Fall of Long-Legged Beast

In Genesis we find not one but two human origin tales. The first account we are given is in Genesis Chapter 1. In that account

> God said, Let us make man in our image, in our likeness,...So God created Man in his own image, in the image of God he created him; male and female he created them.[94]

In the second creation story in Genesis Chapter 2,

> The Lord God formed the man from the dust of the ground and breathed into his nostrils the breath of life, and the man became a living being.[95]

If you study these closely, it's obvious that the second version is the earliest. Here people account for the process of creation in the same way that they made pottery and other useful items. God, the potter, took some earth and shaped it into a human creation.

The first account in Genesis, however, *God wills mankind into being*. He says, "Let it be so," and it was so! This *willing* of man into being is a more powerful philosophical notion and, therefore, scholars say, the later notion. (And, by the way, please note that Adam and Eve were not the names of two historical individuals. They represent the origin of mankind. Adam equals the first man. Eve, the first woman.)

Are these stories representative of good science? Of course not. Are they powerful traditions? You bet, but only through the *eyes of faith*. The whole point of the stories is to say that our Yahweh is responsible for creating humankind and all that is. And that's all a faithful heart needs to say.

But was that all the tellers and writers of these creation stories meant to say? Remember that these early Hebrews were herders and sometimes gatherers. Around a campfire one night many eons ago some precocious kid like you undoubtedly asked his elders, "Where did we all come from?"

The first answer was probably, "Oh, over yon mountains."

But that kid wasn't to be patronized. "Oh no," he said, his arms sweeping around at all the tents, plains, mountains, and heavens, "I mean where did all people originate? How did we come into being?"

---

94 Genesis 1:27, 28. New International Version. Scholars assign this version to "Priestly writers" and the next version to the Yahwists. See "Commentary," <u>New Interpreter's Bible</u>, (Nashville, Tn: Abingdon Press, 1994), page 340f.
95 Genesis 2:7. New International Version.

The adults sitting around probably looked at each other, rolled their eyes back in their heads and groaned. Finally, one of the elders said, "My child, Yahweh created us and everything that is." At that point everyone sighed in relief. But the child wasn't through.

"How did he do that?" he asked. More groans. Some silently wished little Micah's father would take him to his tent and put him to bed!

After a few moments the same elder told the creation story that had been orally passed down to him from his father, who got it from his father.

The Fall

These creation explanations may have sated the young Micah's curiosity as to the origin of things, but it didn't quell his appetite for answers to mysterious problems. He also noticed how ornery people could be to each other. On another occasion he asked, "If Yahweh created us in his image, does that mean he also kills, steals, and abuses others?"

"Oh, no," replied an elder hurriedly. "God is perfect good."

"So why are we so mean spirited?" asked little Micah.

Everyone sitting around that campfire sighed once again. That boy Micah was, once again, asking embarrassing questions. The tribal elder again took the lead in retelling the ancient story of man's fall from Yahweh's grace. Looking around at all the children and adults, he began.

"You will remember that when I told you about God creating men and women he put them in the midst of a beautiful garden and told them to take care of it. What I omitted telling you was that God told them they could eat from any tree in the garden with the exception of the tree of good and evil."

"Why not?" asked little Micah.

"Because if they ate of that fruit, they would die."

"Wow, where is that tree?" asked little Micah, his eyes wide.

The elder looked around at the others, shook his head as a sign of disgust and said, "Son, if you will just be patient and let me finish the story, you will understand." The boy nodded and looked down in shame.

"Now, where was I?" asked the elder. "Oh, yes. As I was saying, the man and woman were told not to eat from the tree that gives one an understanding of good and evil because they would die. But one day the woman was confronted by a serpent..."

"Why did Yahweh put a serpent in the garden?" blurted out little Micah. Then quickly added, "That doesn't seem like a smart thing to do?"

"Son," pleaded the elder, "don't try to decide what Yahweh should or shouldn't do. He knows what he's doing. God doesn't like a smart aleck. So hush and listen."

"Okay," said little Micah, softly.

The elder settled back down and tried to regain his train of thought so he could repeat the ancient story correctly. "The serpent confronted the woman and asked her if it were true that Yahweh had forbid them to eat from the tree of good and evil. The woman said, "Well, he told us not to eat from the tree in the middle of the garden because we would die if we touched the fruit."

"That's not what you told us happened," challenged little Micah.

"What do you mean?" asked the elder.

"You said that Yahweh didn't want them to eat of the tree of the knowledge of good and evil because they would die."

"And?" asked the elder.

"Yeah, Yahweh didn't say anything about the tree in the middle of the garden or that they would die just by touching it. They had to eat it. So which is it?"

By this time most of the adults sitting around listening were grumbling to their neighbors about Micah's uppity-ness. The elder motioned for all to be quiet, then said, "Little Micah, it does seem like something's amiss, but it's really not. I am trying to cut the story a little short because it's getting late."

"Well, it seems to me that that woman hadn't gotten the message straight in the first place. Is that why gossip is always so inaccurate?"

The adults laughed, then the elder responded, saying, "You're probably right little Micah. But regardless of all that, the serpent told the woman that Yahweh had misled them. "The real truth of the matter," said the serpent, "is that Yahweh doesn't want you to eat of that fruit because your eyes will be opened and you will be like Yahweh, knowing good and evil."

Little Micah looked like he was going to challenge the story once again, but the elder stopped him with an upraised hand. He continued, saying, "As I said, it's getting late. So the bottom line is that the lady went to the tree, thought the fruit looked tasty and ate some. And she didn't die. She was so excited that she talked the man into eating some fruit, and they suddenly saw they were naked and ran to cover themselves."

Another kid blurted out, "Why did Yahweh lie to them about dying?"

"Yeah," cried little Micah, encouraged by the support, "That wasn't fair."

"Now, now," said the elder, as he tried to regain control of the group. "I don't have answers to that. I suspect that Yahweh was testing their loyalty and obedience. They failed the test.

"Well, it seems to me he made some big mistakes," continued the second little kid. "First, he shouldn't have created a backstabbing serpent in the first place. Second, he shouldn't have mislead the people and third, he shouldn't have put a fruit in the garden that would help the people to understand good and evil."

"Enough," cried the elder. "Good grief," he said, looking around at the adults, "this younger generation is surely doomed. They are too much the critics!"

After a few moments everyone settled down and waited to see what the elder would say to these challenges from the kids. "These stories have been passed on from generation to generation from the beginning of our earthly time. Just accept them without questions." He looked around. The adults were all nodding affirmatively. The kids looked puzzled. Finally, little Micah had his hand up once again.

"Yes, little Micah, what is it now?"

"Tell us what Yahweh did when he found out."

Relieved, the elder continued. "Well, it wasn't long after the people had eaten the forbidden fruit that they heard Yahweh coming through the garden looking for them. They hid because of their nakedness.

God finally called for Adam, "Where are you?"

And Adam, still hidden, cried out, "I heard you in the garden, and I was afraid because I was naked, so I hid."

"Who told you that you were naked?" asked Yahweh. "Have you eaten from the tree that I commanded you not to eat from?"

Adam said, "That women you put here. It was her fault. She made me eat that fruit."

A woman's voice was heard from the crowd saying, "And you men have been blaming us women for your weaknesses ever since!" There were snickers here and there.

A man's voice retorted, "Oh garbage, if you hadn't listened to the serpent in the first place we wouldn't be in this mess!" Then arguments broke out all over.

The children watched and listened, until the elder finally yelled, "Hey, shut up! What's the matter with you people? It's only a story, for crying out loud. Now hush."

With that, everyone calmed down, although it was evident that the women were plenty steamed. The elder continued, saying, "Yahweh went to both the serpent and the woman. To the woman he said, 'How could you have done this to me?'

The woman said, 'The serpent made me do it.'

'Aha,' cried Yahweh, as he cursed both the serpent and the woman. The woman's punishment was pain during childbearing and domination by her husband. Yahweh relegated the man to toil and sweat in scratching out sustenance from the earth, then to die."

"So this is the reason that we have to work so hard and why we die?" asked little Micah.

"You got it," said the elder. "But it's also the reason that women are ruled over by men and have a painful time at birth." This latter statement created a furor among the adults as men and women got into heated arguments once again.

Finally, the elder cried, "Stop it! Ya'll go home. Git! Git! This session's over."

And so that's how the Hebrews accounted for the presence of good and evil in the world; as well as the sweat of a man's brow, the historic domination of women by men, and death. It's a great story, but it's one that was never meant to be taken literally. *But you must take it seriously.*

There's *Sin*...and then there's sin

The point of Genesis story is that God created humans for his fellowship. He asked that they obey him. They didn't and the relationship between God and his human creatures has been ruptured ever since. Almost. But that's another letter. Right now let's stick with biblically clarifying human nature by defining the nature of Sin. You need to understand that Sin is one thing, and sin is another.

Biblically *Sin* (capital S) is rebellion against God and refers to the state of alienation and separation that exists between God and a person.

Another way of talking about Sin is to say that it refers to a state of personal anxiety that people experience. Some people say it's a feeling of lost-ness or despair. It's important to understand that this condition has nothing to do with a person's being morally correct in a specific society. Highly ethical and morally upright people experience the anxiety that accompanies lost-ness and despair.

For example, a person can...
- attend church, synagogue, mosque, or whatever, on a regular basis,
- pray daily, or five times,
- give to the poor,
- refrain from cursing,
- refrain from alcoholic beverages,
- refrain from smoking, gambling, etc.
- and generally live a perfectly moral life, and...

still be in a state of separation from the Ground of Being (God).

At first blush this sounds crazy because it defies our society's taken-for-granted belief about the perfectly moral individual. We've historically equated the Christian concept of *Sin* with social immorality; those things people refer to as *sins* (little s). For example, people who don't go to church, don't pray, don't help the poor, and who cuss, drink, smoke, gamble, and generally live their lives in what is considered the darker side of social life are generally viewed as sinners because they *sin*. This is biblically incorrect.[96]

Why is this biblically incorrect? Because it puts the emphasis upon what *we do*, not upon what *God does*. But does this mean, therefore, that a righteous person, which I shall posit as the opposite of sinner, is one who doesn't go to church, pray, doesn't read the Bible or do other things generally associated with righteousness? Nope. That's not correct either.

Briefly, a *righteous man or women is one who has felt God's reconciling love and has acknowledged and accepted the restoration of that sacred relationship with God.* That's it! Period. No qualifications. The Christian witness, which coincides with the experience of millions down through the ages, is that one accepts Jesus as the Christ and is touched by God and is thereby a new person. *(The new person is a euphemism for being reconciled to God, the Ultimate Ground of one's being.)*

I would agree that those who have experienced this divine reconciliation are not comfortable with their old patterns of behavior. For example, a *believer* will probably search out a community of others who have also been consumed by the Word. That is, they will find their way to a church family. They will generally feel driven to help the poor and those who are hurting. They will probably shun former habits that destroy the body and hurt the inner spirit. But, the Christian life is not a bed of roses. One still gets ill, experiences family stresses and tragedy, and so forth.

No Christian, however, does more damage than those who believe they are holier than others. No one likes to be around such self-righteous louts. Taking care of one's own morality is a full time job. Yes, unloving actions are often deeply confounding, whether from others or oneself. But life is complicated and we are all beholden to God's mercy and grace. None of us are perfect. Paul, wrestling with conflict, said,

---

96 John Wesley preached a whole sermon about this, entitled: "The Almost Christian."

I do not understand what I do. For what I want to do I do not do, but what I hate I do. And if I do what I do not want to do, I agree that the law is good. And it is, it is no longer I myself who do it, but it is sin living in me. I know that nothing good lives in me, that is, in my sinful nature. For I have the desire to do what is good, but I cannot carry it out. For what I do is not the good I want to do; no, the evil I do not want to do—this I keep on doing.[97]

It should also be mentioned that all societies have used religious ideas of *sin* as a means of socially controlling the general population. In other words, religious *dos and don'ts* are effective legal devices. "God's gonna get'cha!" is a universal admonition that often stops mischief-makers. Or, "If you do that, you won't go to heaven." Or, "If you don't do that, you won't go to heaven."

Such socially defined admonitions against sinful behaviors are legion throughout the world, regardless of religion. Interestingly, the harshest appliers of these are the religious hardliners in any religious community, commonly known as fundamentalists. Since the Twin Tower's attack in September 2001, Americans have learned a great deal about Islam's brand of fundamentalism. Behavior that is viewed as sinful is clearly defined and harshly punished in Islam. But Christian fundamentalism can be just as oppressive. And there are numbers of Christian cults whose legalistic bondage matches anything found in Islam. Such religious usage shows how evil religion can be. Just remember, *there's Sin and…there's sin.*

Summarily, the Biblical view of humankind is of a creature molded in God's own image and meant for fellowship with Him. Alienation, or Sin, tainted the relationship when humans tried to be their own god. They decided to *do their own thing*. They were the world's first narcissists.

Biblically, the history of God and his creatures revolves around our trying to appease God by offering sacrifices and/or following the Law. But all attempts to earn God's love have failed. Then, in and through the man, Jesus of Nazareth, who lived at a particular historical time and in a particular geographical place, God reconciled humanity to Himself. **This God-Man Mystery constituted the end of the Law, of Sin, and religion.**

Now that you understand more about human nature, the next letter will discuss Jesus of Nazareth. The life of Jesus, or what is historically known as the God-Man Mystery, only makes sense against the backdrop of our human condition.

---

97   Romans 7:15f. (NIV).

SIXTH LETTER

THE MYSTERY MAN

Dear Ben and Grace:

Given the preceding discussion of our estrangement from God, it's time to seek a solution, if there is one. And I suggest there is. I've referred to it on numerous occasions. As I explained in the last letter, the Judaeo-Christian tradition says that we were cut-off, or separated from God because of our disobedience. We want to be our own god. Christianity historically views our human predicament, or condition, as a *state of separation or alienation from God*. The solution to this dilemma has posed a great challenge through the centuries.

Early Depiction of Jesus

The Hebrews believed the answer to our human predicament to be found by adhering to the Law. And most of the world's religions, those *other drains* one can choose to go down, attempt to heal the rift between God and humankind by observing certain behaviors to appease God, such as singing, burning incense, saying certain prayers and mantras, or offering sacrifice. Islam, for example, while sharing a great deal with the Old Testament, focuses on *right behavior* and not creeds.

In contrast, the followers of the post-Easter Jesus claimed that our reconciliation with God did not reside in the Law or any human acts, but *solely on God's grace. And God's grace was* revealed in and through Jesus. In other words, *in and through the God-Man* MYSTERY *God's love declared our separation null and void. We no longer live in a state of separation and/or alienation from God.*

Over the last 47 years I've heard Jesus referred to as (a) just a man, (b) a great teacher, (c) God disguised as a human, (c) a man who was gradually transformed into God, (d) half God, half man, and, (e) in our time a sweet friend or buddy. When pushed, most are not quite sure what to make of Him. Few stop to consider the various historical options, opting instead for a conceptualization derived from their childhood that views Jesus as something of a cosmic Santa Claus, who's always watching and rewards you when you're good and punishes you when you do wrong.

What do we really know about the historical Jesus? As you hopefully noted in previous letters, it is not easy to get a precise snapshot of the historical Jesus since he didn't register a formal resume. The historical, pre-Easter Jesus is overlaid with post-Easter interpretive layers that make a full biography impossible. The earliest layer, or the *original* text about Jesus, as well as the second layer known as *tradition,* are both reconstructions written years after his death.[98] The third, or *evangelical* texts comprise a layer from years 70 C.E. to possibly 110 C.E. There are a number of things we can surmise about the historical, pre-Easter, Jesus from reading the original and traditional writings:[99]

- First, he was a Jew and totally devoted to Judaism. He never entertained the idea of establishing a splinter religious organization, either within or without Judaism.

- Second, he was socially and culturally a member of the *peasantry*. His life, like all peasants, was on a subsistence level and he was unschooled. That is, although a brilliant peasant, he was probably unable to read or write.

- Third, as Borg notes, he was a *spirit person, which means that God was an experiential reality in his life.*[100] His insight into spiritual affairs set him

---

98 See Crossan & Reed, Ibid., p. 36f.
99 There are a number of interesting works that delve into the difficulties of historical reconstructing Jesus. Albert Schweitzer's book, previously mentioned, should be read for its historical value. Among numerous others I would suggest Marcus J. Borg's books, The God We Never Knew, Jesus, A New Vision, and, Meeting Jesus Again for the First Time; see also, John Dominic Crossan & Jonathan I. Reed, Excavating Jesus., cited earlier.
100 Borg, The God We Never Knew, (San Francisco: Harper, 1997), p. 89f.

apart from others. Most precisely, he seemed deeply in touch with the *sacred*. As Borg observed, this spiritual aspect of his life served as the foundation of everything else he was. His spiritualism was intense enough that some viewed him an ecstatic or mystic.

- Fourth, Jesus was a healer and teacher. He manifested the sacred by connecting with people through healing and teaching. He was dramatically iconoclastic because he lived out of a different vision of the sacred than did local priests and teachers.

- Fifth, he was what today some would call a troublemaker. His acts and words challenged the prevailing socio-religious system.[101] If taken seriously his teachings continue to challenge prevailing social systems.

- Sixth, and most important, Jesus spoke of a God that had, heretofore, been somewhat ambiguous.

The pre-Easter Jesus provided a vision of God and human life that was unparalleled. His compassionate God did not demand that any person meet any special requirements in order to be loved and accepted by Him. Any and all persons were urged to know the unqualified love of God and God is knowable without any institutional encumbrances.

As Borg aptly states:

> Cumulatively, taking the pre-Easter Jesus seriously as an epiphany of God suggests a massive subversion of the monarchical mode of God and the way of life (individually and socially) to which it leads. God is not a distant being but is near at hand. God is not primarily a lawgiver and judge but the compassionate one. The religious life is not about requirements but about relationship. God as king has not ordained a social order dominated by earthly kings and elites but wills an egalitarian and just social order that subverts all domination systems. Indeed, Jesus used the monarchical language of 'kingdom of God' to subvert the monarchical model; in the kingdom of God, things are very different.[102]

---

101 See Walter Wink's, <u>Engaging the Powers,</u> (Minneapolis, Minn: Fortress Press, 1992).
102 Borg, Ibid., p. 101.

One may scratch out more of the early layers of writings about Jesus, but these seem to represent the fundamental facts. The *post-Easter* Jesus paints a different picture.

The Post-Easter Jesus

As stated earlier, most of the Gospels are comprised of *traditional* and *evangelical* layers of texts. The bulk of the material is written through the disciples' eyes of faith. Jesus was such an extraordinary person that his early followers had to use mystical and metaphoric language in their attempts to interpret him for others. The substantive meaning of this God-Man MYSTERY raged for five centuries and has erupted from time to time during ensuing centuries— e.g. the Protestant Reformation, the expansive proliferation of denominations, sects, etc.

Quarrels over the meaning of the MYSTERIOUS Jesus or God-Man MYSTERY crop up in every Christian congregation. Any discussion of Jesus by two or more Christians too often ends in an argument and hurt feelings. And that's the way it's been throughout history. Well, not quite. There have been times when one who holds a view that differs from the official version would end up on the end of a roasting spit over a huge fire!

There's little doubt that the memories held by Jesus's followers added luster to the God-Man MYSTERY. They even created some new ones. Today we call that editorial license. Stories of fallen heroes tend to exaggerate characters and, coincidently, the God-Man MYSTERY is no exception. It's true today. News media eulogies about the famous tend to magnify a person out of all proportion to reality. Sometimes I wait to see if the person being eulogized really did walk on water. People still claim to see Elvis!

J. Frank Dobie, the renowned writer of Western stories had his roots in Cotulla, Texas. He spent some time working on a local Cotulla, Texas, ranch during the early years of the twentieth century. Ms. Isabel Gaddis, his aunt and editor of Dobie's book, *I'll Tell You a Tale*, told me personally that one of his kin, a rancher named Maltzberger, once jumped Dobie about his wild cowboy stories, exclaiming, "J. Frank, you know none of those stories are true." To which Dobie reportedly replied, "Well, if they weren't, they should have been."[103]

---

103   J. Frank Dobie. *I'll Tell You a Tale,* (Boston,: Little, Brown and Company, 1960).

If Jesus' followers were challenged as to the authenticity of God-Man MYSTERY surrounding Jesus, I suspect they would have said something similar. Martin Marty quotes R.H. Lightfoot as stating that "For all the inestimable value of the Gospels, they yield us little more than a whisper of [the Lord's] voice; we trace in them but the outskirts of his ways."[104] There is definitely a clear chasm between the wee bit we humans are able to understand and the grandeur of His ultimate reality.

Jesus, for his followers, became equated with God. Briefly the consensus testimony revolved around a *compound paradox*:

> Jesus of Nazareth was the Christ, and as such was
> - fully human and
> - fully God.

All early attempts to interpret this MYSTERY led to debates that raged for centuries until put to an uneasy rest at the Council of Chalcedon in 451 C.E. The resultant creed tried to shore up previously adopted creeds, such as that modified by the Councils of Nicea in 325 and 381. It stated:

> Following the holy fathers we all, with one voice, define that there is to be confessed one and the same Son, our Lord Jesus Christ, perfect in Godhead and perfect in manhood, truly God and truly man, of rational soul and body, of the same substance with the Father according to the Godhead, and of the same substance with us according to the manhood, like to us in all respects, without sin, begotten of the Father before all time according to the Godhead, in these latter days, for us and for our salvation, born of the Virgin Mary, the Mother of God according to the manhood, one and the same Christ, Son, Lord, Only-begotten, in two natures, inconfusedly, immutably, individually, inseparately, the distinction of natures being by no means taken away by the union, but rather the peculiarity of each nature being preserved and concurring in one person and one substance, not parted or separated into two persons, but one and the same Son and Only-begotten, divine word...[105]

---

104 Marty, Martin, Op. Cit., p. 4.
105 Kenneth Scott Latourette, A History of Christianity, (New York: Harper & Brothers, 1955), p. 171.

Here's an example of disciples using all the linguistic devices they could muster to firmly establish the idea that Jesus, although *fully a man*, was also *fully God*. As we talked about this in seminary, I remember saying to myself, "Aw, that just means they didn't know what to make of Jesus. They set up this formula to make both sides happy."

Most of the mainline churches today still use the Nicene Creed, which is a modified version of the Chalcedon statement, as a means of expressing the historicity of Christian belief. These historic creeds reflect the elaborate and sophisticated linguistic constructions of the NT writings. Jesus was a man, but he walked on water, turned water into wine, raised the dead, healed the sick, announced the salvation of sinners, and finally, was himself raised from the dead. What type of man was this? He was *evidently* in a different league from all others.

Personally I have no problems reciting these ancient creeds because I know their history and intent. I can affirm the mysterious reality to which they point. There's nostalgia in knowing that one is participating in a worship drama that has been re-enacted for several thousand years *even though* one lives out of a scientific-modern worldview. But for most who are unschooled in Christian history I suspect the words are unintelligible. This is one of the reasons that modern evangelical sects don't use these historic creeds. As one told me, "That stuff's too Catholic!" Give me a break!

Catholic indeed. What nonsense. To jettison early Church history on the one hand, and then to exacerbate our predicament by deleting the other fifteen hundred years of Christian history is like cutting off one's legs. This historical naiveté is based, for the most part, on the misguided notion that, unlike pre-moderns, *our interpretations are correctly grounded in the New Testament,* as though the English language version is a contemporary product devoid of centuries of editing and translation errors.

How can I know if my theological interpretations are more valid than another's if I am not familiar with other's views and the historical struggle over beliefs? Doesn't make sense to me. By ignoring Christian history we also claim that (a) no one else has ever sought to interpret the Mystery; and that, (b) the Holy Spirit has not acted at any other time but our time, and (c) he has only revealed himself to us and ours. I guess God either took a long nap or was off tending to other parts of his creation.

All this boggles my mind. But what can we say about the post-Easter Jesus? Without arguing the scientific authenticity of any act attributed to Jesus, it seems obvious that

- First, the Jesus, God-Man **Mystery** was of such magnitude that human language has been unable to capture it. How can we presume to talk about the God-Man **Mystery**; that great, "I am who I am," reported in Exodus 3:14;

- Second, his followers believed that *He who created the universe broke into human history in a dramatic fashion* (whether one concludes that Jesus was just a man or a god-like apparition);

- Third, Jesus experienced a personal awakening of gigantic proportions.

- Fourth, His vision of God and the fully authentic life were revolutionary and challenged the prevailing religious ideas of his day;

- Fifth, his followers experienced the same Spirit possession. (Millions down through the century have also experienced this possession.).

Having personally experienced a mysterious, life transforming event, I can attest that it does defy human speech and, ultimately, traditional reality. A **Mystery**, by the way, is a God-Man **Mystery** that is always beyond our grasp, beyond our power of definition, beyond our handling and managing. And the Jesus God-Man **Mystery** in history, worship, in all Christian symbols, art, architecture, music, literature, and our own life experiences, is always **Mystery**. Martin Kahler (1835-1912) said, "ultimately we believe in Christ, not on account of any authority, but because he himself evokes such faith from us."[106]

Yet, once aware of the magnitude of this spirit possession in one's life and how early Christians interpreted social and cultural ways through its aura, it's not necessary to insist that the super-natural events attributed to the man Jesus were in every case literal. But…each must be taken seriously!

One only has to appreciate the profundity of what the early writers and evangelists were trying to express. Again, this is *experiential faith* versus *creedal*

---

106 Martin Kahler, The So-Called Historical Jesus and the Historic, Biblical Christ, (Minneapolis, Minn.: Fortress Press), p. 87.

faith. Faith statements use metaphors, aphorisms, and other linguistic devices to dramatize what words cannot freight. We still find ourselves sharing with the early Greeks the idea that **Mystery** always involves miracle and the supernatural because we view reality as having two distinct levels, essence vs. existence, infinite vs. finite, transcendence vs. immanence, and the natural vs. the supernatural. Either-or is our rule.

The church will not do well, in my opinion, trying to evangelize 21st Century people by demanding acceptance of a Jesus history loaded with a literal God-Man **Mystery**. To do that is to ask people to sacrifice their intelligence. But, if a person really needs to believe that Jesus did all those supernatural things, so be it. Again, God's compassionate love and acceptance is totally devoid of any one's intellectual assent to any of that.

Jesus reportedly told the thief dying on the cross beside him that he would join him in paradise after the man cried out for help in his pain. He didn't ask him about his theology, religious behavior, or what he thought about any of his historical actions. Or again, Saul of Tarsus, later renamed Paul, was seized by what he describes as a bright light on the road to Damascus on his way to arrest some of the Jesus sect followers. He claims to have had a conversation with *a voice*. The voice reportedly asked Saul why he was persecuting him. When Saul asked the voice to identify himself, the voice supposedly said, "I am Jesus…"[107]

Notice that the voice didn't ask Saul for his religious credentials. He didn't ask him if he believed any stories or any creeds, if he had been a good boy (he had been a real stinker), nor anything else. Jesus Christ barged into Saul's life without invitation. No religious resumes were asked for in either of these cases. And so it has always been and continues to be.

It's scandalous that Jesus's God loved and accepted people in such condition as Saul, isn't it? Let me emphasize again that the NT witness makes sense to me. Does it make scientific sense? No. Nor do I demand this of it. One who has experienced the *Mystery* reads the stories about Jesus and cries out, "Yes, yes, I experienced what you experienced and are trying to put into words!"

The New Testament message, briefly stated, is that **God's *clearest manifestation of himself* was in and through the life and death of Jesus of Nazareth. It is not the only manifestation of God, but the clearest.** It's impossible to claim that

---

[107] Acts 9

God is not up or out there but here, in, and all around us, and then argue that He restricted His revelation to the Christian disciples. That logic doesn't fly.

But, one may ask, what is one supposed to make of the statements in the NT that Jesus is the *only way*? Remember that the writers who penned these words were positioning the Jesus God-Man MYSTERY against the Platonists and other philosophies and religions of that period. Early Christian writers borrowed a great deal from the Platonists in order to interpret the Jesus God-Man MYSTERY in terms they could understand. John's use of the Greek term, *Logos* (Word), for example, was a concept taken from the Platonists of that time, as discussed earlier. To speak of Jesus as the *only way* was to point to the Sacred, or Divine *Logos*, or *kerygma*, revealed in Jesus. That *Logo* (God) manifests Himself everywhere.

> In the beginning was the Word, and the Word was with God, and the Word was God. (John 1:1).

Basically, God acts as he chooses to act. We disavow God's activity in the lives of all others when we insist that any and all revelation be in our language and reflect our God reality imagery. Again, the emphasis is upon the Word, or Christ's presence. And all people, at all times and in all places, have experienced, and are experiencing, His presence in their lives.

Paul was aware of this. He visited Rome and noticed a statue to the *Unknown God*. He told the Romans that he knew who this *unknown God* was and preceded to tell them about the Word (Logos) that manifested itself in and through Jesus of Nazareth. Paul understood that the God who revealed himself in Jesus also manifested himself to all others. The Romans had simply not understood earlier revelations.

So, the compassionate God manifested in Jesus is the same God that reveals Himself wherever humans are found. He is in and around every single human being, at all times and at all places. There are no unloved and forsaken people in Jesus' image of God.

You are probably wondering why God didn't show himself as clearly to other people? Who says he didn't, or doesn't? First, remember that the media doesn't matter; some people just *don't get it* no matter how it's dished out. Not all have understood the manifestation of God through Jesus. His own religious leaders arranged his death. The disciples were few, although thousands of others saw and heard him. Over the centuries not everyone who has heard about Jesus has believed.

But as one moves around this globe and relates to people of non-Western cultures it is obvious that God is, *in fact*, compassionately present with all people. To demand that all use Christian language and hold Christian beliefs is to domesticate Jesus. What does it matter that a people call themselves Hindus, or Buddhists, Muslims, or other? As Outler points out, "Jesus was not the first authentic self-revelation of God nor the last, but he was the decisive revelation by which all the others can be measured."[108]

Isn't it heresy to suggest that Hindus and others can be of the same vintage as Christians? Not at all. Quite contrary, through the eyes of faith it is gratifying to find that the God of Jesus Christ is present in and with all people. And, remember, it is *God in Jesus* that we refer to, not creeds, words, and institutional trappings. The fact that many Christians view the Church as an exclusive and elite club of the saved or righteous is a result of turning the Jesus God-Man MYSTERY into a religion; a domesticating process that I will take up soon.

In my opinion there are many people around this world who are *unselfconsciously Christian*. I can imagine that such a statement will have a lot of eyes spinning wildly. Remember, Jesus often related to people who were *unclean* for various reasons. In each case they felt a connection with the God-Man. He pronounced them healed or saved. No church relationship was, or is now, necessary. There were no preconditions for God's indwelling love and grace. Through the eyes of faith one can see the God who manifested himself in Jesus also living and revealing himself in people who are not consciously using Christian language and the associated trappings we think of as identifying that presence.

Before moving to a discussion of God's nature, it's important to deal with the issue of Jesus as God's sacrificial son. This is a centerpiece of Christian thought for most Christians. But God didn't sacrifice his son for our transgressions.

Jesus as a Sacrificial Lamb

Ritual sacrifice has a lengthy history among most cultures of the world. You will find human sacrifice used as a means to appease the god, or gods, not only in ancient Jewish history but also in neighboring tribes, as well as among most of

---

108 Ibid., 210.

the North and South American Indian populations. The Jews gradually traded human sacrifice for animals. But, old patterns die-hard. So it was easy for Jesus's followers to explain his death as a sacrifice to Jewish listeners. The writer of Hebrews, trying to communicate to a Hebrew community, speaks of Jesus' death in sacrificial terms more than any other witness. He used this sacrificial analogy in an attempt to show that Jesus fulfilled Jewish expectations for the coming Messiah. It was a useful analogy in that historical context, but not today.

Did our salvation really need a sacrifice? Of course not. To believe and defend this is to perpetuate an ancient, preliterate superstition. Given what Jesus taught about a compassionate God, it doesn't make sense to entertain the notion that he needs a sacrifice to accept his human creatures. To some early Christian disciples, Jesus's death as sacrifice is connected with a notion that he *paid the price for our salvation* or that his death was necessary to balance some *divine scale of justice*. Nonsense. Such an image of the God revealed in and through Jesus is too small. Way too small. The anthropomorphism of God to this low-level is stone-age imagery.

The record seems to be that Jesus's death was plotted by the religious leaders of his day because his vision of God and the Godly life threatened to wreck the prevailing order of things. It was carried out by the occupying Romans to appease the Jewish leadership. That's it.

Professor Albert Outler quotes Halford Luccock as saying that "Jesus wasn't crucified for saying, 'Behold the lilies of the field, how they grow,' but 'Behold the scribes and Pharisees, how they steal.'"[109]

No Divine plot was involved. In other words, God was not playing puppeteer. People acted of their own volition. Nor can one support the notion that because a small group of Jewish religious leaders plotted his death that all other Jewish citizens were involved, as some misguided Christians down through the centuries have believed.

Summarily, for whatever else it might mean, for Christians

- the Jesus God-Man MYSTERY is God's *clearest expression* of Himself;
- wherein God is revealed as a *compassionate, loving* presence in all our lives;
- and that His compassionate love comes to us as *unconditional acceptance*.

---

[109] Outler, Op. Cit., p. 53.

The Jesus God-Man MYSTERY now enables us to talk more clearly about God's nature. My next letter will focus on this task, but I couldn't close this letter without mentioning that *narcissism* in America has led us to great lengths in making Jesus just another *good ole boy*. The following is a true story by Ken Casey of Kentucky.[110] (To get the full impact of the following song you must imagine fiddles playing, toes tapping or dance a little jig.)

> When I got my education, part of it was at the seminary in Louisville, Kentucky. Later, when I was working with some young folks, I realized there was one word that I didn't know how to translate. It was *hallelujah*. I really needed some way to translate the meaning of this word to people so they could understand it better....
>
> One day, I was listening to the radio and heard a Pentecostal preacher say, "Sometimes I get so excited, I just have to r'ar back and say, 'Hot dog, Jesus!'" I knew that was what I was looking for, and that where this song came from:
>
> *Well, He's the sausage of my breakfast,*
> *The sandwich of my lunch,*
> *The meatloaf of my supper,*
> *He's the head of the bunch!*
>
> *He's the frosting on my cake,*
> *The ice cream on my pie,*
> *Sweeter than the honeycomb,*
> *The apple of my eye.*
>
> *He's the gas that fills my car,*
> *That keeps me on the go.*
> *He's the pure white filling*
> *That fills my oreo.*
>
> *Chorus:*
> *He's my Savior, my pride and joy,*
> *Without his death, I'd have no life.*
> *He's my Savior, makes my life good,*
> *He brought me out of sin and strife.*

---

110 Jones & Wheeler (eds), <u>Op. Cit.</u>, p. 116-117.

He's my Jesus, why I want to sing,
He's why I want to shout.
He's my Jesus, I can't hold it in,
That's why I got to let it out:

Hot dog, hot dog, HOT DOG, JESUS!

One of the fall-outs of the Reformation has been the loss of Jesus's divinity in favor of his humanity. This has led in our time to a *sweet, friendly, good-ole-buddy-boy* Jesus that is often sickeningly saccharine. Contemporary fundamentalists have also concocted a Jesus that often comes across as equivalent to a Hollywood movie star, with a sprinkling of mysticism. All this is declared to be Scriptural. I assure you that this human Jesus concept is not Scriptural, nor traditional. It is purely Americana plastic.

You should not forget that the One who declared his love and acceptance of us is the One whose face Moses said we dare not look upon. You should never lose sight of the fact that the historical Jesus Event is about *GOD'S* manifestation. This is why, it seems to me, that we emphasize the Mystery of the **God**-man (note my emphasis upon God). We desperately need to recapture the awesome nature of the Divine in our **God**-man equation.

The Christ God-Man Mystery is the only legitimate answer to our human predicament of separation and alienation from God. The only one who can repair that damage is God Himself, who manifested His love and acceptance through the God-Man Jesus the Christ. We cannot save ourselves. We can only know ourselves through God's knowledge of us and God's revelation to us of that knowledge and love and grace; this was accomplished in and through the act of Jesus Christ. If, as Kierkegaard argued, we could prove the historic accuracy of every detail of Jesus's life, it would not bring a person closer to Christ. And, conversely, if critics could disprove the accuracy of Jesus's life, except that a man did live in the first century who a number of people believed was God in human flesh, nothing of the Christian faith would be destroyed. Kierkegaard, therefore, spoke of Christian faith as *a leap*.

For what it's worth, this God-Man-Mystery constitutes the only *leap*, or drain, I have found worth going down! And with that said, I'll turn my attention to the nature of God in my next letter.

SEVENTH LETTER

THE WHISPER FROM A BURNING BUSH

Dear Ben and Grace, [111]

Please notice that we really didn't have a *clear* conceptualization of God's nature until the Jesus God-Man MYSTERY in the first century. The Old Testament characterization of Yahweh as a voice from a burning bush that spoke to Moses ambiguously saying, "I am Who I am"[112] is all that was available to our early Hebrew fathers. And that was like an historical whisper. Thus, as I stated earlier, the Jesus MYSTERY provides our *clearest expression* of God, such as it is. Quickly, let me add again that it's not God's *only* manifestation in human history, just the *clearest*—and that's a faith statement. The Jesus God-Man MYSTERY enables us, however, to say that God is

---

111   Heading picture, NASA, in public domain.
112   Exodus 3:14.

- an unobtrusively present in the life of every human and
- is pure love, grace, and compassion.

Even so, we still can only talk about God's nature, not his form. Obviously he doesn't speak a particular language, nor does he have a nationality or race. *The form of his Being is totally unknown to us. Totally.* Even the clarity of God's revelation through the Jesus MYSTERY is as though those early apostles got a slight glimpse of the hem of His garment.

Furthermore, as I've continually said, God is *not up there or out there.* Instead God, the Ground of our Being, *is in us and around us...at all times...and in all places.* Forget the traditional OT Monarchial, or Kingly God, who was out in space in a place called heaven. Keep the OT and NT metaphors separate. Jesus taught us better. It's more accurate in the 21st century to think of God as within and around us and He knows every detail of our lives. As we say in the Church, God is *omnipresent* (everywhere). But that's a faith statement no one can prove scientifically.

Martin Buber, the renowned Jewish scholar, emphasized that we only know God in our most honest relations with the YOU.[113] If I ignore YOU, then I ignore God. God (that little old English word we've historically attached to that Being) who has created and sustained the universe is only known through the YOU (whom we might legitimately call "the Other.")

Meanwhile, if God is within me and around me, then why doesn't he make himself known to me? *He does.* At least we make that observation in *faith.* Although an unobtrusive presence in our lives, he speaks to us through our intuitive sense and the voice and touch of other people. Again, His presence is in the form of love, grace, and compassion.

Certainly some seem to have keener intuitive eyes and ears than others, most notably those we referred to in previous letters as *spirit-filled,* for lack of a better term. I use the notion of *spirit* because God's presence is of an ephemeral, metaphysical realm that only can be seen, heard, or felt through the *eyes of faith.* Women seem to be more sensitive to the *Logos,* or Christ. Maybe men camouflage their feelings for cultural reasons.

---

113 Buber, Martin, I and THOU, (New York: Charles Scribner's Sons), 1970.

This leads to other questions, such as: Why do some have more sensitive spiritual eyes and ears than others? Why does one person react to another's pain and grief with compassion while another scoffs? Why, when watching a gorgeous sunset does one person gasp in awe and think of God, while another yawns, turns away and says, "Nice, but it's time for a drink." Other examples of such sensitivity could be listed. I'm sure you will notice others during your own lifetime.

Some people have keener spiritual senses than others. To say this is to maintain the biblical notion of our human predisposition to *play as if* we were our own. This is the fundamental lesson of the Garden of Eden story. When a person is ultimately persuaded of the futility of living life independent of God (the Ground of our Being), then God can be heard in that most dramatic sense that Christians call conversion, or new birth. Until that time God walks with us (*us* means all) *unobtrusively*, continually tapping us gently on the shoulder and waiting for the time when we will acknowledge and accept *and depend on* his presence, love, and compassion.

I know you are also wondering why bad things happen to good and innocent people if God is always with us. That's a question that has always haunted people and a number of good books deal with this issue. Briefly, some Christians talk about God as the *great puppeteer*, which is to suggest that he orchestrates every one's life. If you entertain this idea of God, it leads to a lot of problems. Basically this is not a defensible position. Instead, let me use a human analogy to explain how *God is unobtrusively present* in our lives.

God is with us like a parent or teacher who watches their children at play. Children often have accidents. They break bones, get bloody noses, fall off playground equipment or out of trees, run into things, or get hit by swings, or a miss-thrown bat. The adult supervisor is available for comfort and aid when accidents happen, but generally they don't, and many times can't, prevent accidents, although they like to try. Regardless of age, all of us tend to test reality to an extreme and bad things happen to us. It's tough growing up and it can be tough throughout the adult years.

Like adults watching over children, God is a comforting presence when bad things happen to us. God does not, however, **suspend the laws of the universe to prevent us from harm.** God gave us *free will* in the midst of a universe that operates according to rules. Break the rules and you get hurt. A person who jumps off a ten-story building will either die or break most of his/her bones.

Drive your car into the path of a tornado and you will probably lose your life. And so it goes ad nausea.

How many times has the following conversation taken place between parents and their children?

> Parent: "We warned you what would happen if you did that."
> Child (probably a teenager): "Yes, I know."
> Parent: "Well, why did you do that to yourself?"
> Child: "I don't know."

And like our parents, God whispers to each of us in a variety of ways. At least that's what we affirm through our Faith.

> God: "I've tried to warn you of the dangers of being your own god, but you continue to turn a deaf ear."
> We: "Yes, yes, you are right."
> God: "Are you ready to listen now?"
> We: "Maybe."

Maybe, unfortunately, has been the usual human response to God throughout history.

"But," you ask, "what about the innocent child killed by a careless adult? Where was God? Why did the tornado destroy and kill family members in some house and spare others? Why was Bob's wife killed while driving on an elevated portion of California highway 101 when the earthquake hit and others were spared?

Your great-great grandmother died in childbirth and your great-great grandfather never went to church after that. He could not justify that event with the nature of God as had been presented to him. And Ms. Rosa Gonzalez of Los Angeles lost her son on the Iraqi battlefield in March 2003.[114] According to the article Ms. Gonzalez is angry when she hears parents giving God credit for their sons and daughters safe return. "Didn't my prayers mean just as much?" she asks. She no longer asks God for anything.

---

114 "Mother's faith battered by death of Marine son" <u>Houston Chronicle</u>, Wednesday, August 20, 2003, p. 10A.

Yes, why o' why does God allow such things to happen?

When it comes to understanding *Mother Nature* all one can say is that some people are in the wrong place at the wrong time. For example, why do people continue to build in the same place after floodwaters or hurricanes wipe them out? Or why do people continue to build expensive homes along earthquake fault-lines or on hillsides that are prone to either mudslides or quakes? Are we dumb enough to think that since we are such sweet and innocent people that God will intervene to protect us from Mother Nature?

Do you think that God was behind the sniper that killed an innocent child and others around the Washington, D.C. area in October 2002? Did he choose the people that were on those airplanes that crashed into the World Trade Center in September 2001? *Of course not.* One has to be totally brain-dead to believe that nonsense.

Here's a fact that you and your generation have to live with. Scientists warn that the southern part of the Island of La Palma, off the coast of North Africa, will someday fall into the Atlantic Ocean, creating a mega-Tsunami that will probably destroy much of the U.S. east coast. Will God reach out and stop the Tsunami? Obviously not. And many people will die. Such natural events are part of the ongoing evolutionary process.

I repeat, although God is always present, he does not meddle in human affairs. While we affirm God's omnipotence on the one hand, the Church has historically said that He has, by his own volition, limited his power relative to humankind. He gave us free will. We are free to make decisions and create our future, for good or ill. And please note that he does not have a favorite football, baseball, soccer, basketball, or any other team. It's incredible to hear players give God credit for their win, as though he has favorites. If you accept this it means that you must blame God when your team loses. You will never hear players on a losing team say, "Jesus made ole Joe drop that ball." Or, "We would have won if God had not played on their team." Again, utter nonsense. Superstitious bunk.

Joe Garagiola tells a marvelous story about Yogi Berra, Jimmy Piersall, and God that is very instructive.[115] When Jimmy Piersall came to bat he had a habit

---

115 Garagiola, Joe, It's Anybody's Ballgame," (New York: Contemporary Books, 1988), p. 98.

of reaching across the plate and making the sign of the cross in the dirt with his bat. On this occasion Piersall's team was playing the Yankees and Yogi Berra was catching. When Piersall made the sign of the cross Yogi "came out of his crouch, stepped across home plate, rubbed out the cross, and said, 'Why don't you let God just watch the game?'"

"But," you ask, "what about all those stories where people have been miraculously cured or mysteriously saved from certain death?" The stories are legion. One can find reports of such mysterious phenomena on television almost weekly. But what Americans don't understand is that around this world, in every culture, whether Christian or non-Christian, modern or primitive, there are miracle cure stories. Every ancient Shaman, or witch doctor, can recite such miracles. You can find reports of miracles in every preliterate tribe that's ever lived. Unexplainable events are not confined to Christian populations.

To restate the key issue, *God is always with us but he doesn't intervene*. We have to seek the answer to *miracles*, those creepy events that crop up without a seemingly sane reason elsewhere. We don't yet know all the answers to nature's activities and we don't understand the total complexity of the human organism. As much progress as we've made in medical technology, we still don't have all the mysteries solved. We do know the mind is a marvelously complex thing, whose power is yet not fully understood. But we do know that the human organism has the ability to heal itself if given the proper ambience.

Through mental gymnastics people are able to sleep on beds of nails, pierce the skin with fishhooks and hang from a pole, survive cold or heat beyond anyone's wild imagination, or put the body into a state of such low metabolic rates that the person seems dead. In every human situation some are tougher then others. And there have always been differences in genetics. Survivors have the *right stuff*. The plasticity of the human body is unbelievable. We long understood the body's ability to heal itself if given a chance. Cancer survivor studies show that those who tend to throw it off are those with a stronger will or a significant degree of combativeness. The human mind is capable of all sorts of miraculous, out of the ordinary, feats.

Nonetheless, some people choose to believe that extraordinary events are special acts of God. I never argue with a person who believes in miracles. Although it's a primitive notion, for the most part it generally doesn't matter. It becomes a problem when one relies solely on some god for healing and ignores medical technology. And, if one chooses to believe that God prevents some deaths and not others, it creates a great dilemma. One has to explain how God picks and chooses people. What does one tell the mother whose ten-month-old-baby was crushed to death when the father backed out of the family driveway as to why God allowed this to happen? What great plan justifies such a cruel act? You can't just shuck it off by saying, as many do, with the equally primitive response, "Well, God has a plan that we don't see." So God planned such a cruel act to fulfill some plan that's hidden from his people? To me that's a pre-literate view inconsistent with the *compassionate God as revealed in and through Jesus of Nazareth*.

I suspect there will always be some degree of mystery in life; at least I hope so. As a good friend of mine once said, "There are no well-understood natural solutions to mysterious problems. That's why they are mysterious."[116] Meanwhile, one must not buy into the primitive idea that God is a ghostly creature who impulsively, and somewhat maliciously, suspends the laws of nature to either inflict terrible pain or awesome miracle. One image of God the writers of the New Testament did not offer is of *God the Grand and Capricious Puppeteer!*

In this same vein of thought, an old 17th Century saying crops up in sermons from time to time that covertly blames God for a person's misfortunes. It states, "And there but for the grace of God go I." The speaker is thanking God for prosperity, good health, luck, or what have you. Thanking God in this manner seems, on the surface, to be a gracious thing to do. But, *in reality*, the speaker is seeing God as the causal agent behind everyone's fortune or misfortune, meaning that we are (1) not personally responsible for our plight in life, nor (2) do we live with a universe governed by natural law. God, as master puppeteer, pulls all our strings. So, when I see a man being hauled off to prison and say, "Whew, there but for God's grace go," I am saying that God caused the man's problems? Did God purposefully arrange events so the man would go to prison? Conversely, does God purposefully keep me out of prison?

To think that God manipulates life in this fashion is about as self-righteous and elitist as one can get. This idea follows the ancient pattern that views sickness (leprosy, cancer, and physical deformity) and misfortune as God's punishment. We see the same nonsense cropping up in the Reformation thinking of John Calvin and Martin Luther. To them riches and success are clear signs of God's election. He rewards those who love him and punishes those who don't. There's a gaggle of television evangelists in our own day who hype such

---

116 S.C. Oliver, Department of Anthropology, University of Texas, Austin, Texas; now deceased.

garbage. The contemporary writer, Philip Yancey, reports that he gets letters claiming that suffering is God's punishment. The old superstitions continue.

I suppose that if one were able to go back in time and stand in the crowd watching the man Jesus being crucified as a common criminal, the taken-for-granted logic of most on-lookers would have been, "There but for the grace of God go I." How ridiculous that attitude is to his later disciples. In fact, Jesus' emphasis upon the poor, sick, lame, and sinful as the focus of God's love and compassion turned this primitive superstition on its head. According to Jesus's logic the rich and powerful are those in God's disfavor.

Unfortunately, the pre-Christian idea that those who are rich, healthy, and successful are God's chosen "jes' keeps on keepin' on," as they say. Attend any community meeting where people from a broad socio-economic spectrum are present and notice how the advice from some wealthy person is viewed as more creditable. Generally we consider words from the rich as wiser. Why? Their wealth is a sign of God's election. Wrong!

Summarily, Jesus revealed a loving and compassionate God (Spirit, Christ, Ground of Being). One who loves everyone, but especially the poor, the ill, the abused, and downtrodden. One who is present in every person/s life. Even our enemies. He is in and around us, speaking to us at all times. Sometimes a person hears that still, small, unobtrusive voice, and sometimes not. The problem of hearing God is ours. Usually our *hearing* or *not hearing* measures our willingness to let God be our God.

The Human Response to God's Presence

Last, but certainly not least, there is the age-old question of how one knows a person who has experienced Christ. How do we know a person has affirmed God's presence in his/her life? First, we really don't. As I said in an earlier letter, we were not called to be our neighbor's fruit inspector. We were called to joyously celebrate life with God as our companion. It's important to separate this issue, totally and completely, from God's nature and presence. I say this because God's activity often gets mixed up in the human equation, creating what seems to me a *fuzzy image* of the Christian focus. We can, however, state clearly that one who has experienced the unconditional love and acceptance of Jesus's compassionate God is freed from unlove and enabled to celebrate life and love the neighbor.

Notice that the statement above says nothing about being morally perfect nor pious, which are traditional, taken-for-granted, assumptions about religious people. This is purposeful. One who is Christ-filled does not become God. One remains human, as Paul, St. Augustine and others so eloquently remind us. Those *in Christ* are not always loving. Nor are they always kind. Those *in Christ* hurt others from time to time. And, yes, they often fail the test found in the Lord's Prayer: "…and forgive us our debts as we also have forgiven our debtors."[117] The Christian also fails any and all other litmus tests of righteousness.

You are probably wondering how this could be true. The taken-for-granted view is that Christians are supposed to be morally superior to the non-Christian. While that may be the world's taken-for-granted view, it is not the NT view. The NT view is that nothing we are…or can do…makes us equal with God. We cannot earn God's love and acceptance! It is freely given *in spite of ourselves.* One is never morally superior to any others. Never. If you ever feel morally superior, I suggest that you get some therapy or a heart transplant. Whatever works. Christians are supposed to be humble servants of all.

Again, my previous statement stands: One who has experienced Christ is freed from unlove and enabled to celebrate life to the fullest. The fact that Jesus's God declares his unconditional love and acceptance of humans is all that is required. It's inclusive; no *ifs, ands,* or *buts.* There are no *"but ya gotta do this and that,"* or "ya gotta believe this and that," or "ya gotta act like this or that."

Most people don't seem to grasp the enormity of God's love as manifested in and through the God-Man Mystery. Historically many have thought it scandalous to think that *God loves all humans unconditionally—without any prior acts on their part.* Surely, some have said, a person has to confess, or pray, or something! Nope. Jesus's compassionate God declares His love as unconditional acceptance. That means unconditional acceptance. Hello!

Well, you say, this still doesn't satisfactorily answer the question of why some folks find Jesus, and some don't. First, no one finds Jesus. He's never been lost. That's an example of how petrified our language has become. The truth seems to be that people differ as to how, when, and why they finally acknowledge the Presence that has been there since birth.

Let's muddy the conceptual waters a little bit more. My profound, life-changing experience with the Christ came when I was only nineteen, as I reported earlier.

---

117 Matthew 6:9f, NIV.

There was nothing unusual about the church service. It was a fairly boring dedication of a little church (Ft. Bayard, New Mexico). I didn't do anything to make it happen. I was just sitting in a folding chair minding my own business. In fact, I guess I was thinking about what I was going to do when I got home. The feeling that swept over me was not of my doing. There was nothing about the God-Man Mystery that I can hold up and use to extol my virtue at that time, or any time. Although I was an average teenager wrestling with my future, I had done nothing to deserve God's act. Nor did I call it forth; I wasn't that sophisticated. But it overwhelmed me nonetheless.

Let's go back to Paul's experience on the road to Damascus. He was not seeking anything. In fact, Jesus confronted him against his will. Did Paul have some deep inner doubts and longings? If so, those are not shared with us. He certainly wasn't a "do-gooder" of whom God was proud. And he certainly knew little about the Jesus God-Man Mystery, except these followers of the Nazarene were a bunch of ne'er do-well trouble makers that deserved to be hunted down and locked up.

One can read the autobiographies of any number of past Christians—Luther, Wesley, St. Augustine, St. Francis, and find a great deal of similarity. Although the variety of experiences is amazing, the one underlying characteristic is that the Spirit (Christ) freed them from their own antics toward self-justification and/or self-righteousness. God's unconditional love and acceptance was so overwhelming that they had a hard time believing it. The rest of their lives were certainly not anyone's model of moral perfection as the world defines such, but they all celebrated God's unconditional love and acceptance. This affirmation and celebration of life is the key characteristic of one *in-Christ*.

In addition, there seems to be a *guilt-meter* in those who are in-Christ, which is sometimes missing in those who are not in-Christ. Acts of unlove, or ungrace, trigger painful guilt pangs in Christians. For example, I often hear people who consider themselves Christian using hate language. They will talk about hating this person, this cause and those people. They often hurt others. But in each case there's an acknowledgement of guilt. They know such behavior and attitudes are against the Divine Spirit and they are repentant.

Further, it seems to me that those in-Christ are marked by a special humility that's generally lacking in others. I think this results from an existential knowledge that personal worth comes only from God and not from who we are, what we have, or what we've accomplished. A Christian knows deep down that he or she is loved *in spite of the self*. That's a humbling bit of knowledge.

Summarily,
- The God revealed in and through Jesus is pure love and grace.
- He is compassionate, not angry and vengeful.
- While He's present in everyone's life at all times and in all places, He exists there unobtrusively.
- God does not punish us. We punish ourselves by making bad decisions. The most damaging decision one makes is living without a relation with God.
- God manifests himself throughout the universe and we see and hear him whenever we sense love, grace, and compassion.

Another of the key characteristics of one who has been captivated by Christ Jesus is the ability to *discern God's presence in the every-day life of the world.*[118] In other words, one can see God's presence in the most mundane acts of human life, whether in the kitchen, field, office, marketplace, city council meeting, classroom, tavern, or church.

I've not mentioned *prayer* in all the above, but I believe in prayer with the following stipulations. First, we obviously don't tell God anything he doesn't already know. Second, I've already argued that he doesn't suspend the laws of nature or interfere in our activities, no matter how badly we often wish he would. Authentic prayer doesn't seek to get God to manipulate events or natural causes. It does enable one to sense God's unobtrusive presence and hear more clearly His whisper of love and compassion. It focuses one's attention on critical issues. Answers to pertinent concerns are most often generated under such conditions. Please don't view prayer as a means of calling down a cosmic *bellhop* in the sky or divine *Santa Claus*.

Now let's see what happens to Christianity when we, in our inanity, *domesticate* Jesus. We do this, it seems to me, when we demystify the God-Man **Mystery** and turn it into a religion. My next letter will discuss this taming or domesticating process.

---

118 I'm grateful to William Stringfellow for this insight. We had a close association back in the 1960s.

EIGHTH LETTER

THE END OF RELIGION

Dear Ben and Grace:

In light of the preceding I would like to suggest that *Christianity is ultimately the end of religion* as generally understood. I am aware that this goes against the currents of historic, taken-for-granted views, but now and then it's helpful to think outside the box. Briefly, my argument is based on the simple facts that

1. *Christianity refers to <u>God's activity.</u>*
2. *Religion refers to <u>human activity</u>.*

This seems to me an extremely important distinction. To reiterate the *Good News*, the early Christian witnesses said that in the Jesus God-Man MYSTERY, God revealed himself in a most dramatic fashion. So dramatic was the manifestation that many of the disciples believed *God had become flesh*. That's dramatic in any language.

Furthermore, the early church fathers stated unequivocally that

- God's act in human history declared his love and acceptance of all humans, not just the Jews.
- His love and acceptance was *unconditional* and *in spite of* humankind's willful disobedience.

If you study the NT carefully, it seems obvious that this salvation God-Man Mystery declared in and through Jesus was <u>*of God*</u>. Man *was not* the key actor in this drama—unless one focuses on the fact that people killed the God-Man. So we have nothing to be puffed up about. In fact, this God-Man Mystery is such an awesome mental barrier to climb over that people in all ages have had difficulty accepting it. The mental and emotional hurdles are numerous.

The first difficulty for 21st century people is accepting the fact that the One who created the universe and is of spiritual substance…became a human! This was not, however, a difficult mental task for pre-modern people.

Second, and most difficult for people in all ages is the declaration that God's love and acceptance is *unconditional*. This idea flies in the face of everything we've been taught, as discussed in an earlier letter. Humans everywhere and at all times have felt strongly about punishing wrongdoers. "If you do the crime you gotta do the time," as the saying goes. By contrast, the God revealed in Jesus of Nazareth disagrees with us. He loves and accepts *all humans just as we are.*

As you probably have learned by now, proper behavior has always been taught by using negative and positive sanctions (punishments and rewards). Religious tenets have been the most fundamental whip for attaining appropriate behavior. Some tenets have been extreme. For example, in Europe during the Middle Ages many acts, including that of incorrect belief, could get one tortured and burned at the stake. Priests who accidentally spilled the wine during the Eucharist would have some fingers cut off! Many Muslim societies cut off hands of thieves and heads of adulterers. And, as you probably know, in Puritan New England during the 17th and 18th Centuries, common misbehaviors could land one in the stocks, be branded (forehead, arm, or hand), or dunked in public (used for women, generally), or other such painful humiliations. Interestingly, the New England practice of sentencing misbehaviors to a stroll about town wearing a sign around their neck stating the nature of their crime is making a come back in some towns in contemporary US.A. Furthermore, in early America, if you nodded off in church, you would get slapped-up-side-of-the-head by a self-righteous elder in the back of the sanctuary wielding a long pole. Today you can find groups organized under the Christian banner emphasizing all sorts of prohibitions—from no dancing to no blood transfusions.

Just about the time I think I've *heard everything*, a new group crops up through the media that pushes the limits of extremism further. If a person wants a group that calls itself Christian but lives in ice caves in the Antarctic, eats only sea snails, howls at *the aurora borealis* (northern lights) six times a day and all night on Sundays, prays only in an unintelligible language understood only by the sea gulls, prohibits clothing, doctors, lawyers, marriage, kids, watermelon, skis, boats, lights, and all written material, they will probably find it. If not right now, just wait a few years. So much for religious communities. I prefer to live in a secular society, thank you very much! Besides, nations can't commit to God, only individuals can. Nonetheless, and most important for our purpose, every society has some boogie-man story that says, in effect: "If ya don't behave the alligator god's gonna eat ya up." In the Christian context we scare people with the thought of going to a fiery place called Hell.

The Hebrew Bible is replete with stories of God punishing his people for their disobedience, starting with the Fall in the creation stories. Then a Jew from a little drink-water town called Nazareth comes along and says *that's all wrong*. Instead, he says that *God is pure compassionate love*. To add insult to injury, the early Christian writers declared that God's love and acceptance is free and unconditional to all. Whoa, wait a minute! Talk about thinking outside the boxes!

Whoa, indeed. We humans don't like playing second fiddle, even to God. And we don't appreciate being told that our age-old traditions are just superstitions. Furthermore, this free and unconditional acceptance stuff offends our sense of justice. We prefer to "Hang 'um high and hang 'um good."

You bet! As if the vision of God as pure love and compassion isn't scandalous enough, the Jesus God-Man MYSTERY teaches that even if we do good things—give to the poor, attend worship, pray, don't smoke or drink, abstain from sex, don't wear makeup or sexy clothing, don't curse or chew tobacco, and generally do good doesn't add one whit to God's love or appreciation for us. These acts, in and of themselves, have no merit in God's eyes. In other words, there is nothing any of us can do to earn God's grace. It's freely given *in spite of ourselves*.

Alas, our attempts at righteousness are totally useless. Satirically all the fun in life is gone. Gee whiz, just when we were getting it down pat. We were having so much fun killin' folks for wrong belief or cuttin' 'um up (literally) for doin' all those things we would have loved to do but were afraid to do. Now, how are we going to lord it over our neighbors and scare our children into obedience? Jesus took our toys away.

Jesus's compassionate God who loves all humans *in spite of who we are or what we do*, created a huge dilemma for us all. The historical result has been our inability to cope with the resulting application of God's unconditional love and acceptance. Sure, we pay lip service to the idea. We get teary-eyed when the idea is mentioned in church, but freeze up when we realize that all our praying, church attending, and giving to the poor, and other such worthwhile acts. won't buy one a cup of coffee in God's kingdom. And we are chagrined to find out that God's unconditional love and acceptance is extended to all those dirty, sorry, no-good rascals out there that we would like to whip up on.

But never mind. We humans always figure a way around such *inconveniences*. Even some of our early Christian ancestors felt the unconditionality and universality of God's love was offensive. They attached *conditions* to it. You know the ones. They always start with words like, *but or if*. It generally comes out as, "Yep, God loves sorry ole Joe (or Mary), *but* not unless he/she repents." Or, "God won't love you *if* you don't confess." And this means that *we want to see something* out of ole Joe or Mary that shows us they've changed. We adamantly refuse to accept the unconditionality of love and acceptance as revealed through the Jesus God-Man M**ystery**.

So, we turned the Jesus God-Man M**ystery** *and God's unconditional love into a religion,* with beliefs, rules, numerous acts and paraphernalia and so forth and so on. And in so doing we effectively *domesticated Jesus* and eliminated the mystery from the *God-Man event.*

Did we ever. Every church has a series of *litmus tests* that people must pass in order to show they're one of the accepted. In other words, we may say that God loves and accepts everyone, but we dictate the terms and conditions of other's God relation. People who want to be in our Jesus tribe (church), must pass *our* test, go through *our* initiation rites, and adhere to *our* beliefs. And obviously we cloak our rules and tests with Jesus language to make them palatable, but *the focus radically shifts from God's acts to ours*. We've replaced the old Jewish laws with our own. And the idiot I noted in the first letter who goes about America spreading hate of gays in God's name is the worst of the worst of such religionists!

Christianity Becomes Another Religion

We humans are notorious religion creators. Studies by sociologists reveal that all religious institutions have similar career tracks. They began with a charismatic figure that creates the vision and establishes a following. Once that figure is gone, the followers recreate the vision and rules. This process gradually leads to an established institution, with increasing labyrinths of rules and procedures. Down through the ages many have noted the cruelty that all religions foster.

Once Jesus was gone and the first disciples's interpretations of the God-Man **Mystery** was in our hands, we wasted little time turning that event into a religion. In support of this view, Karl Barth refers to religion as our effort to hide from God. Dietrich Bonhoeffer, the German pastor who was hanged by the Nazis, followed Barth and insisted we needed to create a religion-less Christianity. Unfortunately Bonhoeffer didn't live long enough to develop the content of such a Christianity.

*Fir*st, in any religion the focus is upon human acts that are supposed to appease, and thereby manipulate, the deity (the domestication process).

Second, there's always the *gotta-do* stuff in every religion. In addition to all the traditional elements—going to church, praying, giving to the poor, not cussing or spittin' tobacco on church grounds, nor drinkin', and other such proscriptions, we continue to add to the list of do's and don'ts. When we are really stressed out we ask: "What would Jesus do?"

To ask what Jesus would do in any human situation betrays a person's religious orientation (as opposed to Christian). It shows that a person is looking to be like God, which has been our human predicament since Eden. Interestingly, the answer always supports the speaker's cultural notion of *right behavior*. Jesus was God incarnate, not a sweet, ideal moralistic American. He certainly did not please the Synagogue leaders in that time, and it is doubtful he would please Christian leaders in our time. Once again, such an emphasis misses the vital point of the *Good News*.

As I've often said, the God-man **Mystery** is about God reconciling the world and not about Jesus creating a new set of legalistic behaviors by which we can claim either (1) equality with God or, (2) God's love, or (3) feel self-righteous. The person who has experienced the God of the God-man **Mystery** doesn't ask, "What would Jesus do?" Such people already know their lives are accepted and they act out of gratitude and celebration in every human situation.

Third, the *gotta do* stuff is pinned to the tail of the idea that if you don't do certain things then bad things are going to happen. *Fear* becomes the whip in the hands of the religious person because the mysterious aspects of life are scary. And, boy, have we made Christianity scary! The common, every-day, taken-for-granted worldview of Christianity continues to be an admixture of a world inhabited by spirits, some good (angels), and some bad (demonic ghosties and ghoulies). The people complaining about Satanism, the number 666, and other such superstitions are little more than medieval religionists. Religionists say that God will protect you from the *ghosties and ghoulies and long-legged beasties and things that go bump in the night if you behave*. You will be rewarded by going to heaven. On the other hand, if you're not good…the demons will get you and you will go to a scary place called Hell.

There's a story about a young boy whose grandmother took him to church on Sunday and the preacher preached for way over an hour. The little boy squirmed on the hard pew as long as he could, then asked his grandmother, "Are you sure this is the only way to get to heaven?"[119]

Fourth, every religion defines acceptable religious acts. For example, a Christian may go fishing on Sunday and read some scripture and say a prayer while doing so. That's seems like an admirable event, but the church says that such behavior does not substitute for going to the church building and participating in the formal worship on Sunday morning. In other words, God is not pleased with one's worship on the banks of a lake or trout stream on Sunday morning. Or the golf course. And there are oodles of other requirements attached to being a devout follower, depending upon one's denomination or sect.

You will often hear someone say that God blesses one for doing something good. I've long wondered about that. What do I get for giving a few bucks to a person begging on a street corner? A gold watch? What do I have to do to earn a Mercedes-Benz? Or, I've always wanted to have a nice big cabin on a mountain somewhere in the Rocky Mountains. How many good deeds does it take to get one? Then when I stop and think that Jesus' obedience landed him on a cross, my head spins.

Fifth, all religious acts are tied to a set of beliefs that justify both the acts and the institution itself.

Sixth, religions create sharp social boundaries in every community. It becomes part of the *we vs. they* baggage that organizes life. The drill is easily recognizable. People of one religious group generally *shun* the adherents of other religious

---

119 Loyal Jones & Billy Edd Wheeler, <u>Hometown Humor, U.S.A.,</u> (Little Rock, AR: August House Publishers, Inc., 1991), p. 110.

groups (a topic I'll discuss in greater detail in a future letter). The mischief arises when one religious group believes that another's beliefs are mumbo-jumbo. The supposedly righteous group slips into an elitist way of thinking that quickly justifies the abuse of others. For example, Christians have often declared war on numerous groups that were labeled as savages or infidels. American Indians were red skin devils. Or again, there are Christian conservatives who hate gays, abortionists, Muslims, and others.

True, we've stressed religious tolerance over the years as our nation's religious pluralism increased, but this is a relatively *uneasy truce* in most cases. Jewish Synagogues, Islamic Mosques, and Afro-American churches have all been pilloried and defaced across this nation. Some Christian (I use this term loosely here) TV evangelists ridicule other religions regularly. It doesn't take a large socio-economic quake to unleash the hatred and bigotry lying dormant beneath our religious skins.

Seventh, religious practitioners feel a strong emotional commitment to their religion. This is usually expressed as protecting one's metaphysical god/God. Nothing in human existence is as fiercely held as religious commitments. The protection of one's god/God has provided sufficient justification to do all sorts of evil things to others. Millions of people have been slaughtered down through the ages in the name of Christ, Allah, or the alligator god. It boils down to a battle between our religious tribe versus their religious tribe. The attack on the World Trade Center on September 11, 2001, was an expression of this type of religious fervor.

Summarily, Christianity began as a response to the Word clearly revealed in the Jesus God-Man **Mystery**. *This God-Man* **Mystery** *marked the end of religion, by virtue of the fact that it was all about God's act, not humankind's.* Christ is continually manifested through experiential encounters in human lives. The Pentecost event described in Acts 2 is the example.

When the early disciples tried to figure out how to respond to the Jesus God-Man **Mystery** bad things started happening. The Jesus God-Man **Mystery** gradually took on religious trappings. At first these early Jewish disciples understood themselves as part of the Synagogue crowd, albeit with a significantly different focus. They entered into the life of the Synagogue with a totally new understanding of God and self. God was the one revealed through Jesus as unconditional love and acceptance of humankind, who had freed them to celebrate their human existence without fear of the purity laws. They knew they were loved and accepted in spite of their shortcomings. And they waited for the final Judgment Day. Which never came.

As time passed and the final judgment did not arrive, they tried to figure out how to live in this world with their newfound freedom. They fought over the Jewish purity laws and whether new Jesus converts had to be circumcised and adhere to these. The early Christians gradually put on the garb of religiosity. However, to their credit and Paul's leadership, most kept the focus on God's act. After a century or so that focus faded and gave way to stricter rules, new creeds, and a monstrous religious bureaucracy, which I will note in ensuing letters has been largely repressive and abusive. *That's what religions do.*

When the focus shifts from God's act to our rituals and beliefs, the Jesus God-Man MYSTERY evolves into a religion. And the transformation of the MYSTERIOUS *Word* into a religion means the domestication of the Man-God, which is always what humans have done with God's revelations.

But I urge you to keep your eyes on the Jesus God-Man MYSTERY and His unconditional love and acceptance of you. Celebrate life as a great gift from Jesus Christ. Manifest love in the midst of a world of vengeance and hate. Your life will be rich and you will be obedient.

NINTH LETTER

FROM BARBARISM TO RENAISSANCE
500 C.E.–1500 C.E.

Dear Ben and Grace,

As the sixth century C.E. opens, the Roman Empire has already started to disintegrate. The roots of decay can be found in the 5th century. We also find that whereas the *Council of Chalcedon* (451 C.E.) had settled the Christological issue, it didn't silence the opposition. Dioscorus and his cohorts out of Alexandria continued to stir things up by demanding the Church change and accept the *one nature of Jesus Christ*. It took several more Councils to put the issue of Jesus's nature to an ultimate rest: Either two natures, fully God and fully human, or one nature. So there was Constantinople II, in 553 C.E., Constantinople III, in 680-81 C.E., and Nicea II, in 787 C.E.. Chalcedon 451 C.E. idea of two natures continued to prevail. Outside that central issue, the focus revolved around the idea of a Christian society. The return of the Christ was no longer imminent, the Church was here to stay. Energies were devoted to figuring out how the Christian society was to be developed.

The ensuing tug of war between rulers and pontiffs pitted Clovis, Pepin, Charlemagne, Otto I, and Barbarossa against Popes Gregories, Innocent III, and Boniface VIII. The dialogues between these rival parties took place within the context of a *theocracy* and the stammer of unfaithfulness and limited abilities was notable.

Monastic orders developed what Martin Marty calls "an unlovely edge (as in Dominicanism) or a fragmenting inclination (as in Franciscanism)."[120] But, that's not the whole story. Marty sums up the period well when he notes that despite the profound failings of a majority of the main actors during this period "the lisp of the dialogue and the limp of the friar were human witness of human intent to follow the divine will."[121]

Christian Theology During This Historical Phase

Jesus' humanity, although spelled out in the New Testament as clearly as his divinity, continues to puzzle every generation. Everyone following Chalcedon said, "Okay, he was both God and man. But our salvation hangs on the fact that he was God, so that's what we'll focus on." Big mistake. Upon Jesus' humanness hang our ideas of human ethics. <u>When Christian ethics is melted into the salvation mystery the resulting product turns out to be otherworldliness, asceticism, or Puritanism</u>, and hence, the loss of the early evangelist's notion of reality (the *kerygmatic* reality).

Chalcedon, you should know, forces us to confess two natures in one single identity. In other words, Jesus's humanity is identical to our humanity. How to sensibly explain such a paradox continues to give the Church difficulty. One should not view *Jesus the man* as some kind of super*man* (Apollinarianism, Nestorianism). Instead, Jesus's humanity should be viewed as God's way of identifying Himself with us that enables us to identify ourselves with Him in the process of reconciliation.

Professor Outler points to some art that demonstrates this problem.[122] The *one nature Jesus* idea held by Dioscorus and his kin can be seen in eastern Orthodox icons where the crucified Jesus is portrayed dead but his eyes are wide open. This symbolizes Jesus's divine nature. Theologically, the medieval historical period went back to this and sacrificed Jesus's humanity on the altar of his divinity. They held that Jesus's humanity was not really anything like our humanity. This notion still exists. A person may agree that Jesus was truly human, but then wrinkle up the nose and hedge by saying, "Yeah, but he was different. He was sinless." This is a way of saying that Jesus's humanity was somewhat of a sham, a not so subtle magical display. And this is what

---

120   Marty, Martin, Op.Cit., p. 91.
121   Ibid.
122   Outler, Op. Cit., p 167.

Dioscorus and his followers claimed hundreds of years ago. But the Council of Chalcedon in 451 and subsequent councils labeled such thinking as heresy. Bluntly, it is not Christian.

In this argument about Jesus's nature rest the seeds of worldly discontent to this day. It's easy to jump to the conclusion that this world, and all that's in it, is sinful, sinful, sinful. Then one can run for the monastery or, like some contemporary fundamentalists, pray for God to take us away from all these sinful, evil people. Or, one can hide from the world inside a church!

There were a number of stalwart, independent thinkers during the thousand-year period, 500 C.E. to 1500 C.E. Although I identified St. Augustine with the 5th Century C.E., his theology continued to influence Christian thinkers during this vast period—and does to this day. There was also St. Francis of Assisi, Bernard of Clairvaux, and Thomas Aquinas, and many others. Each of these men *stressed* Jesus's humanity in Chalcedonian terms, fully God and fully man. This is found in St. Francis's piety, Bernard's mysticism, and St. Augustine's theology. In these cases one finds Jesus's human connection in full. All manifested the ethical life of love as revealed in Jesus Christ.

Unfortunately, the beliefs of laity and of the rank and file of Church leaders didn't coincide with that of these great men. That story constitutes an embarrassing chapter in Christian history.

The Historical Postscripts

Theological issues took a back seat during the years from 500 to 1500 C.E. The Roman Empire came tumbling down during the 5th and 6th centuries as rulers and pontiffs struggled for control. Most historians believe the Empire got too large to manage. It attempted to protect and maintain approximately 10,000 miles of borders while being assaulted by barbarian invaders. Others insist that demographic factors led to Rome's fall. As non-Romans migrated to the city the populations gradually assimilated until the original Roman population was only faintly visible. In the West, Rome inherited Celts, Gauls, and Germans. In the East, non-white Mid-Easterners and North Africans moved in. The truth may be found by combining a number of these factors.

The influx of non-Romans included the spread of Islam from its Arab roots in the south (Islam covered almost as much geography as the Roman Empire by the 8th or 9th centuries) and groups that were called *barbarians* from the north and northeast (started in the 4th century). The *barbarians* have historically been seen as cultural inferiors. Interestingly, the barbarian cultures readily adapted to the Roman culture over time, but the whole process further weakened an already eroding Roman Empire.

Briefly, by the 5th century Germanic people were establishing their presence in the West. There were Visigoths in Spain, Ostrogoths in Italy, Burgundians and Franks in Gaul, Vandals in North Africa, Angles and Saxons in Britain, to name a few of the most notable. If that wasn't troubling enough for the Romans, Mongols from Asia, led by Attila, took possession of the eastern European area from the Caspian Sean north to the Baltic. The Germanic groups (Goths), by the way, brought to the table some values that some historians credit for being the roots of our notion about individual freedom.[123]

The gradual loss of territory to barbarian invaders and the lure of greater wealth in Egypt and western Asia led the Empire's center to be shifted to Constantinople. This shift was most notable during Constantine's reign in 4th Century. If you will remember my earlier letters, Christendom's fault lines were early drawn between the Greek speaking churches to the east, gradually known as the Byzantine Empire, and the Latin language Roman Empire in the west. While the Roman Empire fell apart in the west the Byzantine Empire flourished in the east, expanding down the Nile River delta area into Nubia and Ethiopia and into Arabia and China.

The Eastern Orthodox Church

The Byzantine Church is historically known as the Eastern Orthodox branch of the Church. The ultimate split between the Latin and Greek Byzantine Church culminated in 1054 C.E. To this day the Coptic (Egyptian) church continues to hold to the *monophysite's view* of an exalted, but not fully human Christ, a direct affront to the Council of the Chalcedon formula of *fully God, fully man*. The second clash between West (Roman Church) and East (Orthodox Church) revolved around *iconoclasm,* the use of images so important to worship in the Eastern Church to this day. The two-dimensional images of Christ, his mother and the saints, with their patinas of gold leaf and multi-colored jewels décor is powerful.

---

123   Barzun, Op. Cit., p. 225.

Don E. Post, Ph.D.

The issue that finally sealed the split between East and West revolved around Photius, the Patriarch of Constantinople in the late 8th century. His appointment was constantly fought by Rome. The East's conception of having five equal patiarchates consistently clashed with Rome's claim to uniqueness and centrality and Photius' accusation that Rome had arbitrarily inserted the *filioque* clause (that the Holy Spirit proceeds from the Father and the Son) into the Nicene Creed. The original formula spoke of the Holy Spirit only as proceeding from the Father. The Greeks were not averse to saying that the Holy Spirit proceeds from the Father through the Son, but objected to saying *and the Son*. Last, the Eastern priests were permitted to marry.

As I stated earlier, the Greek Church didn't roll over and play dead. In many respects it had a more ethical tradition than did the Latin Church. It could also be said it was more catholic and more apostolic than the Western Church. Unfortunately, those of us in the west have largely ignored the Greek Church. Its history is not usually considered when chronicling *our history*—and we are the poorer for it.

One should not conclude, as some have, that the Roman Empire disintegrated because of *immorality,* unfaithfulness to God, or some other such nonsense. Even though St. Augustine and other thinkers over the centuries have used this excuse, they were wrong. Tis' not true. Every illness or painful event was interpreted as God's punishment for sinning. The demise of a state was no exception. But no human institution is forever. All are prone to mismanagement and/or bad judgments, greed and abuse. This is not to condone or ignore any perceived moral vacuum during this vast period of time. The debauchery at all levels of life at this time is mind-boggling. This includes the life of clergy.

You will find that this period, until at least the 11th or 12th centuries, is often referred to as the Middle Ages, or Medieval Age, while the Dark Ages generally refer to the 5th through 10th centuries. The one-hundred-year period of 450 to 550 seems to have been the particularly cruel times. Government ceased to function; Greek speakers were only found in Constantinople, the capital of the Eastern empire; few could read; and everyone had to protect and fend for themselves. Feudalism evolved as a civil construct to provide some measure of protection. The population of Rome had plummeted from one million in the second century to less than 50,000 by 550 C.E. Schools were generally gone, as were teachers. Europe seemed like a wasteland.

The fact that historians always write and speak of the Middle Ages in the plural indicates the period can be divided into several phases. Also, some historians believe labels associated with this vast period to be ethnocentric hindsights.[124] Fact is, while Rome was no longer able to provide assistance to the outlying areas and many cities had to go it alone, all was not doom and gloom. Political and social structures may have been in relative chaos and human energy generally consumed with subsistence survival, but not all stuck their heads in the sand and cursed the night. There were some very interesting things taking place, especially after the 10th Century C.E.[125] And, for my purposes it serves little to argue about the merits of what one calls this period of European life. All agree that the years 500 to 1500 C.E. reflect profound *stagnation* and eventual flowering.

Obviously it's difficult to summarize any thousand-year period of human history, much less this one. Nonetheless, I will try to provide a sufficient historic sketch so you can grasp the general flavor of this vast period.

Medieval Common Life and World View

Manchester suggests that

> ...if value judgments are made, it is undeniable that most of what is known about the period is unlovely. The portrait, which emerges, is a mélange of incessant warfare, corruption, lawlessness, obsession with strange myths, and an almost impenetrable mindlessness.[126]

This sounds pretty harsh, but is, unfortunately, a fairly accurate portrayal of the period. It's seems incredible that a people with all the historical resources of the Greco-Roman periods could lose so much so fast. There was little or no science and little civilization up until the 12th and 13th centuries—in spite of some bright points. Generally the only ones who could read and write were clergy sequestered in monasteries. Intellectual endeavors were laughed at. Reportedly, a cardinal of the Church attempted to correct the Latin usage of Emperor Sigismund in the 15the Century and the Emperor replied: "*Ego sum rex Romanus et super grammatical*"—as king of Rome, he was above grammar.[127]

---

124 Barzun, Ibid., Harris, Op. Cit.
125 Ibid., p. 225f.
126 Manchester, Op. Cit., p. 3.
127 Ibid.

Life in general was especially difficult for those on the bottom rung of the socio-economic ladder, the peasantry, which comprised the overwhelming majority. Life was marked by incessant plagues, famines, and personal abuse. Villages were comprised of fewer than one hundred people and situated eighteen to twenty miles apart. It is estimated that 73 million people populated the European continent, approximately 20 million within what was called the Holy Roman Empire.[128] People did not wander far from their birth settlement, so even neighboring villagers  were aliens. In addition, the surrounding area was a large and dangerous forest inhabited by bears, wolves, outlaws, and imaginary demons. Murders were common and the perpetrators were rarely caught.

Daily life was characterized by backbreaking labor and personal violence. Hence, people kept close to home and even married local villagers. This sedentary life style led to the development of local dialects that made understanding one's neighbors difficult.

Personal and communal hygiene was almost unknown. It has been said that the masses generally bathed at birth and death. The average life expectancy was around thirty years.[129] The average man was a few inches over five feet tall and weighed 135 pounds. Women were shorter and lighter.[130] Childbirth resulted in a short life span for women. If a woman was lucky, she might live into her mid-twenties.

Peasant housing was crude. A compound housed an extended family and all their livestock. Everyone, including visitors and some of the animals, slept on the same large bed, the mattress of which was inhabited by vermin. Some didn't have beds. Instead people slept on a straw mat on the floor. Some didn't have blankets. The same clothing was worn day after day. Social graces were lacking. Manchester paints the following picture:

---

128 Ibid., p. 45.
129 Ibid., p. 55.
130 Ibid..

...table manners were atrocious. Men behaved like boors at meals. They customarily ate with their hats on and frequently beat their wives at table, while chewing a sausage or gnawing at a bone. Their clothes and their bodies were filthy. The story was often told of the peasant in the city who, passing a line of perfume shops, fainted at the unfamiliar scent and was revived by holding a shovel of excrement under his nose. Pocket-handkerchiefs did not appear until the early 1500s, and it was mid-century before they came into general use. Even sovereigns wiped their noses on their sleeves, or, more often, on their footmen's sleeves. Napkins were also unknown; guests were warned not to clean their teeth on the tablecloth. Guests in homes were also reminded that they should blow their noses with the hand that held the knife, not the one holding the food.[131]

Sounds like a *redneck's* dream! Such was life for the bulk of Europe's population during this period. Eighty to ninety percent lived in these small, isolated villages and grubbed out a living from the land. Towns were geographically larger and denser but just as filthy as villages. The largest towns, Paris, Naples, and Venice, had approximately 150,000 souls, and that's a gaggle for those unhealthy conditions. London had a population of around 50,000. After the 10th Century an improvement in general economy saw an increase in cities, each designed and managed better. Hygiene had improved.

A large, turret-lined wall surrounded each town, and a Cathedral's tall spires announced its presence. Inside were narrow alleys, barely wide enough for one person to traverse. Shops and dwellings opened up on these alleys. Those structures of three, four, or five stories were homes of wealthy merchants. Each  story was constructed so that it hung out over the alley below. It is reported that people of the upper floors could reach across and touch each other. In this manner the alley below was protected from rain. But, alas, the alley was also the dumping ground of refuse of all kinds.

---

131 Ibid., p. 57.

Medievalians were Christian in name only. The only part of the God-Man M**YSTERY** they heard came from the local priest, who was not literate and as much a victim of local superstitions as his parishioners. All education and books (first hand written copies, later printed) were controlled by the Church. The Bible was written in a language none but the priest could read and the Latin incantations at mass were foreign to all. Their worldview was not dramatically different from that of dreaded pagans or barbarians. Christianity was purely an institutional category during these centuries. Medieval life was organized around the Church. No one was aware of the early evangelist's experiences and understanding of Jesus, the God-Man. And with the exception of the few theologians mentioned earlier, it could be argued that none of the clergy, bishops, or popes understood the Gospel![132]

Gurevich tells a story that originated with a 14th Century English preacher named John Bromyard, who met a shepherd and asked if he knew the Father, Son and Holy Spirit. The shepherd answered, "I know well the father and the son, for I tend their sheep, but that third fellow I don't know. There's nobody in our village with that name."[133]

The common, every day, taken-for-granted view of the universe was that the world was an immovable disk around which the sun and all other heavenly bodies revolved. Heaven was *up there* above the skies somewhere, inhabited by angels and cherubs. Hell, a flaming inferno as characterized by Dante, lay beneath the soil somewhere. That's just the way it was, and anyone who didn't understand such things was thought a fool.

Everyone, including priests, bishops, and popes, (with a few notable exceptions) believed in sorcery, magic, werewolves, amulets, and *ghosties and ghoulies and things that go bump in the night*. Manchester characterizes the medieval worldview:

> ...and every child was taught—that the air around them was infested with invisible, soulless spirits, some benign but most of them evil, dangerous, long-lived, and hard to kill; that among them were the souls of unbaptized infants, ghouls who snuffled out cadavers in graveyards and chewed

---

[132] See the excellent discussion of this issue in Aron Gurevich, <u>Medieval Popular Culture: Problems of Belief and Perception,</u> (London: Cambridge University Press, 1997).

[133] Ibid., p. 218.

 their bones, water nymphs skilled at luring knights to death by drowning, dracs who carried little children off to their caves beneath the earth, wolfmen—the undead turned into ravenous beasts—vampires who rose from their tombs at dusk to suck the blood of men, women, or children who had strayed from home. At any moment, under any circumstances, a person could be removed from the world of the senses to a realm of magic creatures and occult powers. Every natural object possessed supernatural qualities. Books interpreting dreams were highly popular.[134]

In addition, the Church adopted many pagan habits from the mass of barbarian settlers. Pagan festivals became Christian festivals—Easter, Christmas, All Saints Day, etc. The search for holy relics believed to be imbued with mystical powers, became a grand hobby. Sainthood, abhorrent to early Christians, arose and continues to this day. Augustine (5th Century C.E.) was against the adoration of saints, but local priests and laity adamantly believed that evil spirits could be driven away by calling upon saintly powers.[135] Magicians and astrologers continued to proliferate. They are still present in the 21st Century.

One would hope that by the 21st Century all the medieval superstition would have been washed out of our systems by science and technology. But I've often run into college-educated people who share a number of these medieval worldview traits. Astrology is still popular. Vast numbers of twenty-first Century people still believe in *ghosties and ghoulies and long-legged beasties and things that go bump in the night.* This includes devil worship, the use of amulets and magical items, superstition of all kinds (and some the ancient world never heard of!), and other such nonsense.

The Church's Common Role in Common Suffering

What was the Church doing all this time? Unfortunately, it mirrored the superstitions, immorality, and cruelty of civil society. As one reads the history of the Church during this period it's obvious that laity, priests, and prelates totally

---

134 Ibid., p. 61.
135 Manchester, Op. Cit., p. 14.

misread the New Testament—if they read it at all. The Christ of the *kerygma*, that kernel of testimony about Christ from the earliest evangelists, is not recognizable, with a few notable exceptions.

What happened? First, the barbarian invasions led to mass tribal conversions. The Church was unable to assimilate through proper education the resulting masses. Second, the church took over civil duties, becoming judge and jury of people's behavior, which often led to fights with princes and kings. Third, the Church levied taxes and accumulated property, becoming the wealthiest and most powerful institution on the continent. Wealth and power corrupted Church officials at all levels.

The emergence of Christian Roman Emperors (most notably Constantine in the early 4th Century and Charlemagne in the 8th) was both a help and a hindrance.[136] All kings and princes tried to control the Church, thereby compromising the Gospel. They effectively tainted the Church with power alien to the Gospel.

Manchester characterizes this sad chronicle:

> At any given moment the most dangerous enemy in Europe was the reigning pope. It seems odd to think of Holy Fathers in that light, but the five Vicars of Christ who ruled the Holy See during Magellan's lifetime were the least Christian of men: the least devout, least scrupulous, least compassionate, and among the least chaste—lechers, almost without exception. Ruthless in their pursuit of political power and personal gain, they were medieval despots who used their holy office for blackmail and extortion. Under Innocent VIII (r. 1484-1492) simony was institutionalized; a board was set up for the marketing of favors, absolution, forged papal bulls—even the office of Vatican librarian, previously reserved for the eminent—with 150 ducats (about $3,750) from each transaction going to the pontiff. Selling pardons for murderers raised some eyebrows, but a powerful cardinal explained that "the Lord desireth not the death of a sinner but rather that he live and pay." The fact is that everything in the Holy See was up for auction, including the papacy itself…[137]

Nonetheless, Christendom *as an institution* expanded during the medieval millennium. There was an upsurge starting around 950 C.E., for example,

---

136 Latourette, Op. Cit., p. 63.
137 Manchester, Op.Cit., p. 37.

which lasted for several centuries. A few good and honest popes, bishops, and priests appeared periodically. They were just too few and far between. Aristocrats of all sorts sought the Church's blessing or divine authority to legitimate their rule. Many led crusades to the Holy Land in order to win Papal approval and favors. Without question, life was dominated by the Church, from baptism, marriage, and burial.

A focus on the medieval criminal justice system, managed by the Church, is another chapter in the whole sordid story. Property offenses were harshly dealt with. Offenders might have their heads shaved, be ordered to leave their families, be assessed a prison sentence, be sent on a pilgrimage, have ears cut off, or eyes gouged out. Generally punishment was excessive and cruel. A number of non-church related events profoundly affected medieval life, and some changed world history.

First, in the category of catastrophes, there was the *great plague.* Genoese sailors evidently brought the plague to Messina in October 1347. By the time authorities discovered the sickness and drove the sailors out of Messina it was too late. The plague spread throughout Sicily. It reached Italy and France in early 1348, and from there to the rest of Europe. Many villages were wiped out. It is said that a third to half of Europe's population was wiped out.[138] Monastic communities were also wiped out. One of the results of the plague was the mass destruction of Jews throughout Europe. A population fed ignorance about the Christian faith for centuries turned on Jews as scapegoats.

The second significant event was the development of the movable printing press in 1448 by Johannes Gutenberg Gensfleisch (he preferred his mother's maiden name). He did this with the help, by the way, of his typesetter, Peter Schoffer. The men published the Bible with 1,282 outsized, double-columned pages.[139] Presses quickly spread throughout Europe. Manchester observes that as great as this achievement was at the time, its real value took time to be utilized. Literacy amongst the clergy increased, although it was not acceptable to write, or now publish, in the vernacular. This had always been seen as a means of controlling knowledge, which, in the hands of the masses could lead to revolution. How right they were!

---

138 Bishop, Op.Cit., p. 307.
139 Manchester, Op. Cit., p. 95f.

Don E. Post, Ph.D.

The Monastic Movement[140]

As stated earlier, the monastic communities kept the faith (such as it was) alive during these many centuries. They were a *dim*, but important, *light* in a sea of darkness. The act of withdrawing from society in a metaphysical pursuit predates Christianity, however. The Essenes, authors of the famous *Dead Sea Scrolls*, were well known ascetics predating the time of Christ. Christian monasticism reportedly began in Egypt in 305 C.E. by St. Anthony, who started by organizing disciples into ascetic groups. It rapidly spread throughout the Byzantine Empire and then to Europe. The Christian monastic movement really flowered during the Middle Ages. Old monastic forms gained renewed vigor as new ones emerged. They became the repositories of literacy in Europe.

You are probably wondering why any sane person would join a monastery and subject the self to poverty, silence, hard labor, celibacy, and hours of worship. That's a good question. However, in the case of the Middle Ages it's probably less a brainteaser than it is in modern times. The blurring of the moral and ethical lines between religious and secular life was blatant. It was almost impossible to live a saintly life, as then conceived, by participating in the world. Daily life was full of treachery. The decision to join a monastery was not, it seems to me, a mighty leap. The monastic life, for the most part, removed one from the daily violence and chaos that characterized medieval life. Most important was the prevailing belief that one could attain that purity of soul that led to eternity only in the monastic setting. In my opinion this is a misunderstanding of the New Testament. As I stated earlier in the letter, *when Christian ethics is melted into the salvation mystery the resulting product turns out to be otherworldliness, asceticism, Puritanism, and hence, the loss of kerygmatic reality*. In short, don't think of the salvation mystery (God's activity) in the same breath as a person's ethics or good works!

Yet, even monasteries did not necessarily protect one from the brutality and chaos of the day. Monasteries were often overrun and looted by ravaging hordes of barbarians, Muslims, Magyars, and others. And Monasteries had to contend with church and civil authorities that siphoned off wealth for their own use. Secular authorities often appointed heads of monasteries that had little use for the monastic life other than to use it as a source of income. They

---

140 Pictures in public domain, University of Texas Library.

would move in with their wives and families. Monastic life was not always a happy place.

The famous Benedictine Rule espoused by Benedict of Nursia in the 5th and early 6th centuries C.E., stressed austerity and worship. His Rule spread, and by the time of Charlemagne's death, the practice was fairly wide spread.[141] He founded the monastery at Monte Cassino, half way between Naples and Rome. (Interestingly, it was occupied by the Nazi during WW II and well demolished by the American troops. It has since been rebuilt.

One of the most famous monasteries was at Cluny, north of Lyons, France. It became the monastic model for several centuries, thus the forbearer of the Franciscan, Dominican, Jesuit, and Cistercian orders. Cluny eventually lost its vigor. In fact, as each monastic group emerged, it eventually succumbed to success and its accompanying wealth, which prompted a new monastic order. Still the best minds migrated to monastic communities, which left the secular realm devoid of its elite thinkers. A significant and unfortunate *brain drain*.

Throughout the Middle Ages the monastic communities were responsible for writing literary duplicates (primarily of biblical letters) and teaching. Some monks even traveled from town to town teaching and caring for the needy. Historians claim that ninety percent of our Latin classical writings are copies from the early Middle Ages.[142] Some institutions contributed to a higher culture, namely *universities* and their *arts curriculum*.[143] For example, at the Sorbonne, Oxford, and Cambridge a group of teachers provided the arts curriculum, which had to do with what we now know as mechanical arts. Our modern universities are rooted in this era.

The renewed burst of optimism, energy, and prosperity that marked the 10th to 11th centuries stood in stark contrast to the innocuous 5th and 10th centuries. Those living during these latter centuries shook off the hibernation of their forefathers and came alive once again. True, the political turmoil swirled around them, but life continued getting better. A merchant class emerged from the ashes of the dark years, and progress was made in metallurgy, transportation, and efficient energy conversions. The newly emerging capitalism, albeit primitive, gradually sent shock waves through the existing feudal system. A

---

141 Latourette, Op. Cit., p. 333.
142 Barzun, Op. Cit.; Bishop, Op. Cit., Latourette, Op. Cit., Manchester, Op. Cit.
143 Barzun, Op. Cit., p. 228f.

new kind of harness led to the horse-drawn plow and carts. Mining techniques improved and enabled Europeans to reach deeper veins of copper, iron, tin, and lead ores. Agricultural surpluses began to emerge, which joined developing technology in driving the establishment of new cities.

In science and technology the latter medieval period expanded beyond that left from the Greeks and Romans. For example, Franciscan Roger Bacon (1214-1292) is credited for his development in optics, but he also foresaw the steam engine, aircraft, telescopes, and microscopes. He lectured at Oxford and at the Sorbonne.

Other developments often overlooked and mentioned below are:

- Advances in physics, math, astronomy, and geography, are credited to Cardinal Nicholas of Cusa. He also contributed to advancements in philosophy and jurisprudence.[144] Cosmologists credit him for his idea of the cosmos as continuous rather than a myriad of different spheres of materials.
- The evolution of early Latin into Medieval Latin, which Barzun calls a "medium exact expression."[145] It is responsible for modern sense of the subject-verb-predicate structure.
- The development of the water driven mill enabled continuous grinding and metal shaping capability.
- The encyclopedia shows up in the 8th century and is still with us.
- Hundreds of artifacts, such as utensils, jewelry, plates, armor, firearms, movable type.

We should also add that the medieval period developed the clock and handed down our concept of time. It is significant that one can visit Europe today and see that early intelligence in bridges, houses, and churches. The craftsmanship is superb. The architectural design masterful.

Unfortunately, the Church dug in its heels at any and all threats to its absolute control over the lives of men. Its most notorious means of keeping people in line continued to be personal abuse. The most pronounced period of abuse is called the *Inquisition*, from the Latin word *inquirere*, which means *to look at*.

---

144 Barzun, Op. Cit., p. 230.
145 Ibid.

Don E. Post, Ph.D.

The Inquisition

Heresy has always been a problem for religious organizations and has deep roots in the OT. The author of Deuteronomy 13:5 insists that false prophets or dreamers (of heresy) must be put to death because they preach rebellion against God. Religious leaders assume they are responsible for passing on *right belief* untarnished and undefiled. However, while concerned with maintaining the integrity of the *kergyma*, the God-Man M*YSTERY*, early Church fathers counseled removal of the heretic from the Church, *not death*.

For example, in a letter to Titus in the church at Crete, the writer encourages care in the handling of heretics.

> But avoid foolish controversies and genealogies and arguments and quarrels about the law, because these are unprofitable and useless. Warn a divisive person once, and then warn him a second time. After that have nothing to do with him. (3:9f)

Like so much of the early Church's counsel, this finally gave way to physical punishment during the middle ages. The Church couldn't stand much deviation and there were occasional executions of heretics prior to the 13th century. These were legally institutionalized in 1231, when Pope Gregory IX established a commission to *inquire into heretical matters* in France.[146]

In 1478 Ferdinand V and Isabella imported the inquisitional apparatus to Spain as a state managed operation. They turned their guns on converted Jews and Muslims. The infamous head of this terrifyingly cruel operation was a man named Torquemada. He even tried to put an end to St. Ignatius Loyola! As unbelievable as it may sound, the Spanish Inquisition did not end until 1820.

Until the Spanish Inquisition cranked up in 1478, those most effected were in central and southern Europe. The Scandinavian countries missed the Inquisition altogether. And, although the Inquisition ebbed and flowed throughout the targeted area, it was cranked back into high gear in the 16th century as a means of combating the Reformation, which I will discuss in my next letter.

A lot of the period literature does a good job of explaining the Inquisitional machinery as the Church's best effort to maintain purity of the Faith. Again,

---

146 Empress Theodora put a number of heretics to death in the 10th century.

however, I betray my own ethics when I say that in my understanding of the God-Man **MYSTERY** there is no justification for man's inhumanity to man—in any age.

There are numerous ways the Inquisition suppressed the minds of men. One of the most notable, however, is that of Galileo, whose open acknowledgement of the Copernican idea that the sun, not the earth, is the center of the universe led to his house arrest. Galileo died at his home near Florence in 1642, still contained. I guess one should be grateful he wasn't beheaded. I'm sure he was!

Let's take a giant historical leap and see how the Inquisition would play out in a confrontation with the historical Jesus. How likely is the following dialogue?

> A disciple: "Hey, Jesus, there's some people here saying some things that are contrary to your teaching."
>
> Jesus: "What? How dare they! Go get 'um, put 'um in prison and if they don't recant in a few days, put 'um on a rack and stretch 'um until you pull their limbs from their bodies."
>
> Disciple: "O, boy, we can do that. But is that all we can do to 'um?"
>
> Jesus: "Well, be creative. Some of 'um are too stubborn, jest burn at the stake or cut their heads off"
>
> Disciple: "Boy, O' boy, O' boy! We're gonna have a bunch a' fun!"

Does that sound like the Christ communicated in the *kergyma?* Is this the language of the God of compassion?

I've already mentioned the key role that St. Agustine, Bishop of Hippo, plays in Christian thought to this day. Other key thinkers during the period from about 500 to 1300 were:

- Boethius, born in Rome around 480 C.E., emphasized that God could be accessed through reason;
- Peter Abelard, born in Britanny in 1079, emphasized reason above faith;
- Thomas Aquinas, born in Aquino, Italy, around 1224 C.E., tried to resolve the conflict between Augustine's City of God and City of Man. Augustine saw these two as in conflict and Aquinas tried to resolve what

he saw as contradictions. Whereas this had been seen as Augustine's *two truths,* Aquinas tried to postulate the unity of truth. He died without achieving his goal.

The Renaissance

As bad as life during the early Middle Ages had been, a few lights shone at the end of the historic tunnel. Humanism, rooted in the 12 century, leads to a flowering of thought in the 14th and 15th centuries.

A new order of things was further signaled by afore mentioned new towns that popped up across the European landscape in the 12th century. People began to be secure behind town or city walls and lived in more comfortable dwellings. Churches were still built as the city's organizational hub and provided the organizational center for society. Agriculture had improved with the advent of crop rotation, the plow, and use of draft animals. Food became less expensive. A sizable merchant class developed. Trade goods moved along improved secure routes. Families began to send their sons to universities to learn to read and think (always a dangerous social activity). Trade with the East replaced the idiotic crusades. State lines became fairly solidified, so kings and princes weren't as prone to battle for more land. Islam had been pushed out of Italy and Spain. Christendom (as an institution) now extended from Greenland to Slavic Eastern Europe.

A new spirit of learning reared its head as men began to value the ancient classics. These scholars had grown tired of *scholasticism* and its focus on theology. They were labeled H*umanists,* for their interest was upon man, not God. They focused on man's ability to do, to act, and to create. It is here one finds the initial seeds of modern day concepts of *individualism* and *secularism.*[147] The Humanists prized the works of Cicero, Pliny, Virgil, Ovid, to name a few. Reason and logic became the tools of good scholarship. These tools have served us well over the centuries.

In addition, Renaissance painting is said to be the high point of 15th Century art. Notable writers include a number who straddle the lines between the 15th and 16th Centuries, such as Erasmus, Petrarch, Shakespeare, and Montaigne. Thus began an age of literacy that was completely absent throughout the earlier

---

147   See Barzun, Op. Cit., p. 44f.

centuries. And, most important, it was no longer easy for Church officials to intimidate and silence dissenting views. The Genie was out of the bottle!

These intellectual stirrings were enjoined by rising feelings of nationalism and, unfortunately, but not unexpectedly, racism. Nationalism is a key ingredient in the grab bag of *we-isms* and always harbors racist sentiments that can ignite a bonfire of hatred. One only has to view nationalism during the last few centuries to see how these demons work in tandem.

Erasmus (1466–1536) [148]

One of the key Humanists to change the course of thought was Desiderious Erasmus, born in Rotterdam in 1466. He became a priest, then a monk. His mental appetite was enormous. He did not share the closed theological mentality of the Scholastics and read the classics and everything else he could get his hands on. By 1500 he was known throughout Europe for his scholarship. His knowledge of Green was unsurpassed and he translated many of the Greek classics into Latin. In the process he began to realize that St. James' Latin Vulgate (ca. 400 C.E.) translation was heavily flawed and set to translating a new one from the original Greek. The Latin version, along with a commentary and improved Greek version became public in 1516, just a year before Luther's famous posting on the All Saints Church doors. Erasmus's influence has reverberated through the centuries.

Given all this resurgence it may seem that the 12th through the 15th centuries were more of the same old political chaos. That was not the case. These late medieval centuries were *relative stabile*, but still continued to increase in population in spite of droughts, floods, and accompanying famines. Occasionally an aroused peasantry revolted, seeking relief from their suffocating circumstances—most notably the uprisings in Italy and France in the mid-1300s and, of course, England's Peasants' Revolt of 1381. And there was the Great Schism within the Roman Church in 1377, when there were two and three popes, a farce that continued for almost a century.

Then, in 1320 was born one John Wycliff, who became a notable theologian at Oxford, England. He made the first Latin to English translation of the Bible, which became the King James Version of 1611. Embarrassed by the Roman

---

148 Picture in public domain, University of Texas Collection.

Church's Great Schism, Wycliff grumbled aloud about Rome's claim to ultimate authority. He contended that:

- the Bible had all that one needs for salvation,
- the Church was abusive,
- the idea of transubstantiation should be abolished,
- confessions should be ended,
- penance should be thrown out,
- the use of holy water should be abandoned,
- relics should not be venerated.

In brief, Wycliff exemplified an extreme form of heresy before Luther's time. His ideas were shared by a large number of laity. In Wycliff one finds the Protestant idea of *individualism* a century before Luther tacked his theses upon the Wittenberg Church door. Although Wycliff did not found a church, he trained priests who went around England preaching his version of the Gospel. The priests were called Lollards. Wycliff was finally put on trial by King Henry IV, who decided that such heresy would no longer be tolerated.

Wycliff (1328-84)[149]

Lollardry went underground, to emerge during the Reformation years. (Englishman William Tyndale (1494?-1536), a century later, bypassed Wycliff's version and used the Greek version and Erasmus's new Latin version to publish an English version. He had to flee to Germany lest he lose his head. Once printed, copies quickly found their way to England, Tyndale was arrested for heresy and was condemned, strangled, and his body burned in 1536. Weren't Christians a fun crowd to be around?

It should not be forgotten that significant changes had taken place in the east. Constantinople became Istanbul in May 1453, when Emperor Constantine XI died fighting the Ottomans. That ended the Eastern Roman Empire.

By the 13th century the curtain began to fall on a long and sordid history whereby the Church totally dominated (suffocated?) European society, and rising upon a new Europe that could rightly be called incipient modernity. The European landscape during the late medieval centuries was comprised of a large, better educated, and better fed population. There was a revival of Greek

---

149   Picture in public domain, Universty of Texas library.

and Roman literature, led by Petrarch, born in 1304, and his colleague, Giovanni Boccaccio, born in 1313 C.E. Some historians, by the way, consider Petrarch's birthday as a good time line for the start of the Renaissance.[150] These two contemporaries collaborated on reviving the classics and the Greek language. And of course, I would commit a serious historical faux pas if I failed to mention the contributions of Leonardo da Vinci (1452-1519); the egotistical thinker, Pico della Mirandola; Clement Marot (146?-1544); Francois Rabelias (1483?-1533); Geoffrey Chaucer (1342-1400); Michael Montaigne (1533); Shakespeare, born in mid-16th century; and Francis Bacon, developer of the scientific method.

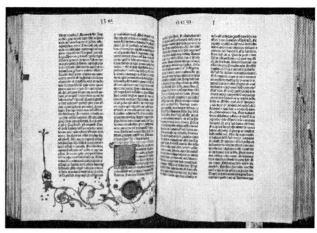

Many intelligent laity were fed-up with Church incompetence and corruption. The grumbling was intensifying. My next letter will briefly sketch the life of the Church during the Reformation and the initial post-Reformation period (1500-1800 C.E.).

The Waning of the Middle Ages

This thousand-year period of the Church's life is a mix of fear and hope. Maybe these traits were balanced, maybe not. It was certainly notable for its extreme contrasts. It affirmed its unity on the one hand and divided itself into East and West. While claiming the inability to err, it ignored the relative nature of being a human institution. While claiming scriptural authority it seems to have ignored good scriptural exegesis.

It should never be forgotten that this was also the age that produced universities, cathedrals and Gothic architecture, turned back the Islamic threat to Europe,

---

150 Charles Van Doren, <u>A History of Knowledge,</u> (New York: Ballantine Books, 1991), p. 130.

developed a pastoral theology, produced great hymns, converted the barbarians, and witnessed the lives of such men as St. Francis and Thomas Aquinas.

In my next letter I will sketch the history of the Protestant Reformation. Unfortunately, Protestants tend to look back and characterize the Christians of the Middle Ages as tiptoeing through the centuries in fear and despair, "heaven-bent on breaking through to new light at the signal of Reform."[151] But God's fingerprints are clear in every age. The faithful abounded. And there were, as Marty points out, "good doctors of the Church in every age."[152] Yet, Church and society were suffering. Night fell.

In my next letter we'll investigate the Reformation period.

---

151 Marty, Martin, Op. Cit., p. 146.
152 Ibid.

TENTH LETTER

THE OPPRESSED BECOME THE OPPRESSORS[153]
1500–1900 C.E.

Dear Ben and Grace,

In the previous letter I sketched a brief history of the Church and society during the thousand-year period of 500-1500 C.E. Obviously I left out a great deal, but your reading can fill in the blanks. Although blessed with a number of creative moments, the Church's many arcane and inhuman activities during the middle ages are embarrassing, but there's no use pretending they didn't happen. It demonstrates how Christians work to domesticate the God Man MYSTERY in every age. (And, yes, I know this is a value judgment from my position in the 20th and 21st centuries C.E. I'll address this issue after I've laid out the Church's history.)

Briefly, for whatever else it did or did not do, the Reformation recovered more fully the Chalcedonian paradox of the God-man MYSTERY, on the one hand, and solidified individualism and emancipation on the other.[154] The masses were freed from at least one version of Church tyranny. This Reformation story gives us something to smile about…and a lot to cry about.

---

153 Picture of "Whipping" from English Newgate Calendar, pub. 1790-1890. In public domain.
154 See Barzun, Op. Cit., for a lengthy discussion of these historical features during the 15th century to the present.

Increasing dissatisfaction with the papal apostolic authority provided the hinge that opened the door to the Reformation. In other words, the reformers found in their own hearts that God's direct witness through Jesus Christ trumped Rome's claimed presumption of apostolic tradition and its monopoly of righteousness. None represents this personal soul hunger as Martin Luther's search for *a righteous God*[155]

Religious Emancipation in Europe

You will remember from my last letter that the seeds of the Reformation were sown in the 12th and 13th centuries and developed strong roots during the 14th and 15th centuries. Martin Luther, frustrated by the Church's historical abuses raised the sword and severed the umbilical cord with Rome in Wittenberg, October 1517.

Erasmus and Wycliff were key players. Intellectuals, meaning most specifically the Humanists, were sick and tired of the Church's suffocating hold over thought, word, and deed and were already primed by Erasmus's witty satire attacking the Church's evil ways. Men from the growing merchant class, as well as local nobles, were weary of the Church siphoning off most of their money. Erasmus, writing after Luther had thrown down the gauntlet, said:

> May not a man be a Christian who cannot explain how the nativity of he Son differs from the procession of the Holy Spirit? If I believe in the Trinity in Unity, I want no arguments. If I do not believe, I shall not be convinced by reason. The sum of religion is peace, which can only be when definitions are as few as possible and opinion is left free on many subjects. Our present problems are said to be waiting for the next Ecumenical Council. Better let them wait till we see God face to face.[156]

A Dominican friar named Johann Tetzel, who was chosen by the archbishop of Mainz to raise money by selling indulgences and letters from the pope forgiving sins carried the fuel that ignited the Reformation fire. Likened to an American frontier-type snake oil salesman, Tetzel claimed that the indulgences he was hawking could even free loved ones who have died and were in purgatory. He

---

155 Marty, Martin, <u>Luther</u>, (New York: Viking Books), 2004. An excellent book on Luther.
156 Ibid., p. 55.

said, "As soon as the coin rings in the bowl the soul for whom it is paid will fly out of purgatory and straight to heaven."[157]

Unfortunately for Tetzel some of the people took copies of their letter to Martin Luther, a monk on the faculty of Wittenberg University. Luther, who had already stated his opposition to the selling of indulgences, responded in the usual academic fashion. He tacked his arguments against indulgences on the door of the Wittenberg Church at noon on October 31st, 1517. Of course, there were other professors' documents there also. But Luther was aware of the annual display of relics shown at the Church on the next day, All Saints Day. Not wanting to leave anything to chance he prepared a circular written in the German vernacular and had it distributed to all those who gathered for morning worship. Then, he sent a copy to the Archbishop of Mainz, the man who had hired Tetzel.

Doors of All Saint's Church, Wittenberg

One would assume that Luther was either seeking election to high office or had a death wish. That may sound silly, but he was a complex man, full of contradictions. A son of peasant parents who physically abused him, he reportedly entered the priesthood because it was the last choice his parents would have approved. His father hated the Church, but believed in Hell, as did everyone in those days. Luther grew up with visions of Hell populated by witches, ghosts, ghoulies, goblins, and all those scary creatures that man is so adept at creating in his vivid imagination. Unfortunately, none of his educational activities rid him of the superstitions accumulated from childhood.

Luther never could shake his childhood demons. That medieval world so full of demons, witches, *ghosties and ghoulies and things that go bump in the night*, comprised his basic worldview. As it did for all. Luther went a step further. He reportedly saw the Devil on numerous occasions. I've found nothing in the literature to suggest that the Reformation did anything to flush the demonic world ideas down the toilet of history. The European worldview continued to

---

157 Manchester, Op.Cit., p. 135.

maintain the notion of a world full of demons. Almost 500 years later it remains prevalent in America! (It should have topped the list of illegal exports to America starting with the Mayflower.)

Briefly, Luther had a lot of support for his anti-papal attitude. These feelings had been bubbling up for many years. Luther and a number of his contemporaries put feet to the prevailing notions. If not, he would have lost his head fairly quickly. Of course, history does not deal kindly with Pope Leo. He evidently failed to take Luther seriously and allocated responsibility for managing Luther to the head of the order, Gabriel della Volta.[158] Evidently Volta didn't understand that he was to put an end to Luther's publications and public speeches. Volta continued to protect Luther.

Martin Luther

As people chose sides, Luther continued to write and publish in the German vernacular. All sorts of Church leaders demanded that he either be censured and removed from his teaching post or burned at the stake for heresy. Luther's list of grievances continued to grow. He came to believe that every man was his own priest and not only opposed the sale of indulgences but the magic of relics, the veneration of saints, some of the sacraments, and called the Holy City of Rome Babylon. It became clear to Luther than few had read the Bible for themselves, so they were totally at the mercy of the Church's teachings.

Most important, however, was Luther's discovery of God's *Righteousness* in Paul's letter to the Romans. Luther concluded that *God's justice* has nothing to do with the punishment of sinners. Rather, God grants His righteousness because He wants to give it. So to Luther Paul's notion of *justification by faith* does not mean that what God demands of us is faith, as if this were something we can conjure up or achieve and which God rewards. Instead, *faith* and *justification* are *free gifts* to His creatures.

The maneuverings of Luther, his supporters, and Church leaders during these years makes for interesting reading. As the pressure escalated it didn't take Luther long to realize there was no way of stopping the increasing public demand for reforming the church. His destiny was set. He was officially declared a heretic and became a fugitive from the Church. He led students and others at Wittenberg University in a book burning. Students burned all the

---

158 Manchester, Op. Cit., p. 145.

books in the library. Luther threw a copy of a papal bull on to the fire. He is quoted as saying, "Because you have corrupted God's truth, may God destroy you in this fire."[159]

The most dramatic and crowing *Reformation moment* came at Luther's hearing, an inquiry set up by King Charles V. Charles was subjected to a great deal of papal pressure to get rid of Luther and other heretics, but he was acutely aware of popular anti-Church sentiment, so he moved cautiously. He hoped that Luther would be tried and convicted at the hearing. Charles V promised Luther safe conduct to and from Worms, the site of the hearing. Yet, to make sure Luther was safe during this journey his followers arranged to have a cadre of Knights accompany him. The contrast between Luther, in his simple monkish robe, facing a body of Church and State elite, all decked out in their peacock-*ish* finery must have been awesome. Manchester describes these folks as

> ...prelates in embroidered, flowered vestments and, second, secular rulers and their ambassadors in the most elaborate finery of the time—short furred jackets bulging at the sleeves, silk shirts with padded shoulders, velvet doublets, brightly colored breeches, and beribboned, bejeweled *briquettes*, or codpieces.... Titled laymen wore coronets, tiaras, diadems; young Charles, presiding on a throne as supreme civil judge, wore his imperial crown; prelates wore miters, and burghers furred and feathered hats.[160]

The collection of Luther's works was piled on a table for all in court to see. When urged to retract his words as written in those books and tracts, Luther hesitated and asked for time to consider the request. Charles gave him a day.

The next day Luther adamantly refused to recant anything that was contrary to Scripture. When the chief protagonist pointed out to him that heretics always excuse their beliefs by referring to Scripture and that biblical interpretation was given by God to ecumenical councils and the Holy See. While the proceedings were conducted in Latin, Luther replied in German as he noted how many times councils and popes had been contradicted. Instead of recanting, as King Charles demanded, Luther spoke that famous line, "Here I stand. I can do no other." He turned and departed the hall, his audacious reply leaving each of the rich and famous agog, I suppose.

---

159 Ibid., p. 159.
160 Ibid., p. 171.

Manchester claims Luther's protective Knights were given orders to kill Luther "if he recanted."[161] What is one to do in such a situation? This threat undoubtedly intimidated Luther to some degree.

There is no doubt that Luther's act of rebellion incensed King Charles V. As Charles moved to neutralize Luther, the populace continued to mobilize. The night the hearing concluded with Luther's abrupt departure, placards appeared all over Worms sporting an image of a simple peasant's shoe, which Manchester states is a symbol of revolution.[162] Luther was hidden in a Thuringian Forest castle known as Wartburg.

Luther left a great legacy of books, position papers, and hymns. But, his most important work was translating the Bible into the German language.

It's important that you view the Reformation period as chaotic. It was. Luther was only one of many reformers. They didn't agree with each other, although they managed to find common ground in opposing papal rule, replacing Latin with the vernacular, opposing the evils of the cult of the Virgin Mary and the use of relics; to name a few of the most notorious elements they fought over.

Luther's followers became known as Lutherans and a new church organization was spawned. But there were other reformists of Luther's renown, such as John Knox of Scotland, John Calvin of France, and Huldrych Zwingli of Switzerland. The key sects that arose out of the ashes were the Presbyterians, Congregationalists, Anabaptists, Mennonites, the Bohemians, and the Unitarians. Then the fun began again.

Luther and his colleague's *protest* against the Church's suffocating control of religious and intellectual life led to all being labeled *Protestants*[163]. Unfortunately this revolt against Catholicism turned into a nightmare for many Protestants. The reform sects turned out to be as obscene as those they had fought against. People

Wartburg Castle

---

161 Ibid., p. 178.
162 Ibid., p. 173.
163 The term "Protestant" came out of a 1529 session of the Diet of Speyer. The Catholic group was asked to rescind a previous act of toleration of Lutherans, but there was a "protesting minority." The Protestant label gradually became acceptable.

who didn't adhere to the new party line or didn't behave *righteously* were publicly executed.

Manchester writes that,

> Peasants would walk thirty miles to hoot and jeer as a fellow Christian, enveloped in flames, writhed and screamed his life away. Afterward the most ardent spectators could be identified by their singed hair and burned features. In their eagerness to enjoy the gamy scent of burning flesh, they had crowded too close.[164]

That's a stellar example of the Gospel of Jesus Christ! But that's not the end of the story. Thousands were slaughtered as the Reformation opened the floodgates of centuries of anger and abuse. Mobs went on the rampage in numerous towns, stoning priests and even women kneeling in prayer.[165] Luther tried to stop the violence, but to no avail. Gradually Luther lost support of the peasants and many elite individuals. Luther tried to calm the people of Orlamunde, but they stoned him and threw mud on him until he retired.[166] The following Peasant's War cost the lives of approximately 100,000 peasants.[167]

Luther may sound like a peacemaker, but he was as intolerant as the next. He believed it was okay to kill someone who didn't have *right belief.* Obviously not all those who took up the sword were committed Lutherans but opportunists who used the movement to extract some measure of vengeance against their assumed oppressors. This is a pattern in most social change movements.

As for losing his movement companions, his loss of Erasmus's support was probably unavoidable. Erasmus, a humanist, hated barbarism, violence, and ignorance. He believed in the goodness of man and his ability to work out his own salvation. Luther, of course, viewed man as sinner and totally dependent upon God's grace for his salvation. He didn't expect much from man.

All Reformists believed in predestination, which held that God had predetermined what happened in life. Man is without a choice. God has one's every move, including where one will spend eternity, all worked out before one's birth. This is especially troubling in the light of Luther's famous tract on

---

164 Ibid., p. 177.
165 Ibid., p. 178.
166 Ibid. 179.
167 Latourette, Op. Cit., p. 724f.

Christian Liberty. Luther, while clearly grasping the all-inclusive notion of God's grace as expressed in the God-Man Mystery, could not make sense of the concept of man's free will. It gave him great anguish.

John Calvin

John Calvin was born in 1509 at Noyen, a small town some sixty miles northeast of Paris, to parents who wanted him to become a priest. He seemed to have a religious bent as a young man.[168] He studied law, was interested in humanism, wrote Latin, knew Greek and Hebrew, and published his first book when he was twenty-three. At Basel, Switzerland, when he was only twenty-six, he published The Institutes of the Christian Religion, one of the best works of the Reformation—if not the best. It's a must reading for any Christian, regardless of denominational commitment. You will want to read the 1559 version, published a few years before his death.

Calvin shared the Reformist belief in the primacy of the Scriptures and felt that the Roman Catholic Church had corrupted its meanings. Scripture taught, among many things, that God transcends all human thought but reveals himself in universal orderliness and Scripture, the Trinitarian formula as explained by St. Augustine was normative for all Christians, God is sovereign over all his creation and, therefore, controls each and every event, Salvation is through Faith (as it was for Luther) and is the work of the Holy Spirit.

Calvin does not resolve the mystery of good and evil in this world, by the way. He cites St. Augustine and lays the blame for evil on evil men, not God. Calvin's most notable theological proposition, however, is what has been called *double predestination.*[169] To wit, some are saved and some are not. And the test of salvation is reflected in the quality of a person's life. The Godly life is found in professing one's faith, leading a pure and righteous life, and participating in the sacraments. Reconciling God's love with His choosing some for damnation didn't seem to cause Calvin the grief it did Luther.

The State, according to Calvin, is to aid the Church in fulfilling its mission. The state should make sure that citizens have sufficient food and drink, prevent anyone from harming the church, provide a favorable climate for good business, preserve peace and generally make sure that all is calm.

---

168   Ibid., p. 752.
169   Ibid., 755.

In 1536 Calvin teamed with a man named Farel in trying to implement the concept of a *sacred city* in Geneva. Ousted from power a few years later, Calvin was eventually reinstalled. Geneva became an intolerable, oppressive caldron of Calvinism. People who criticized Calvin were tortured and some put to death. Life was austere and harsh. Anyone playing or celebrating life, which means they were dancing, singing, gambling, playing cards, hunting, drinking, having sex out of wedlock, wearing lipstick or rouge, and so forth, were punished. First offenders were let off with reprimands, but chronic misbehavers could be beheaded. Attendance at church was compulsory.

Manchester cites the following examples:

> A father who insisted on calling his newborn son "Claude" spent four days in jail;
> A woman who wore her hair an at "immoral" height also spent four days in jail,
> A child who struck his parents was beheaded
> Any single woman discovered pregnant was drowned
> Adulterers were summarily executed.[170]

And the ultimate crime was heresy. Does this sound familiar? It seems to be axiomatic in human history that the oppressed become the oppressors. The only changes the Reformation seemed to bring were the players. The rules didn't change. The Roman Catholic Church, by the way, instituted a new reign of terror in 1542 as a response to the Protestant Reformation and the two religious groups fought each other for control across Europe for centuries. Suspicion still characterizes relations between Protestants and Catholics worldwide. In America in the 1960s a sizable group of *fearful* Protestant ministers fought John F. Kennedy's presidency tooth and nail. The Reformation fears, suspicions, and superstitions continue to live on in our day.

Further Development of Christian Thought

Theologically, Calvin and Luther had a great deal in common relative to indulgences and other such relics of historic Catholicism. Both affirmed the primacy of Scripture and justification through faith and so forth. Luther, however, didn't share Calvin's interest in creating the City of God on earth. Luther's belief in man's sinful nature prevented him from having confidence that man

---

170 Manchester, Op. Cit., p. 191f.

could create the Kingdom of Heaven here on earth. Calvin tried to establish an earthly Kingdom of Heaven and became a tyrant. Luther was right. Human nature is tainted and only God can establish a righteous kingdom. Many contemporary Christians have forgotten this lesson in their zeal to impose their notions of a Christian nation on our country.

While Luther and Calvin agreed on Scripture, the Trinity, man, sin, and grace, and so forth, they couldn't agree on the Eucharist. The Lutherans, while denying the Catholic notion of *transubstantiation* (which means that the bread and wine is transformed into the blood and flesh of Jesus Christ upon the words of the priestly consecration in the Mass) they arrived at a parallel parking site by emphasizing that in the event, Jesus Christ presents himself in his fullness to the hearts and minds of the participants—a psychological transformation. This is, therefore, the early Lutheran doctrine of the *real presence* of Jesus Christ in the Eucharist.

In contrast, the Calvinists emphasized the majesty and infinity of God. In effect they said, it is not possible for the infinite and *wholly Other* to enter into human finiteness. The Calvinist's emphasis upon Jesus's divinity reminds one of the Nestorian heresy that occupied so much of the early Church's time in those first few centuries. Christ's presence in the Eucharist is only spiritual, not real.

Luther popularized the dualism of faith and reason. Luther emphasized the God-Man Mystery by portraying God as hiding himself (*deus absconditus*) from man's continued attempts to domesticate Him. As I understand the Gospel, it speaks of God as always with us, but unobtrusively and of such nature that He is difficult to comprehend. In other words, He is available to those who have eyes to see and ears to hear.

The Protestant Reformation Legacy[171]

First, the Reform movement, for all the good it did, and it did a lot of that, created a situation where the Church splintered into hundreds of churches, alienated from each other by creedal issues. In other words, the Church has never managed

---

171 Space does not permit a treatment of all the key individuals that played a vital role during these turbulent times: Erasmus of Rotterdam, Melanchthon, Bucer, and Huss in Germany, Wycliffe and Thomas Cranmer in England, John Knox in Scotland, Zwingli in Switzerland, those responsible for the rise of the Anabaptists (Blaurock, Grebel, Hoffman), Menno Simons, a Dutch priest who started the Mennonites, and Loyola, to mention a few.

to agree on the meaning of the God-Man Mystery. And so, rather than seeing our unity in Christ's salvation event, we continue separating believers according to a myriad of simplistic beliefs or practices. This practice continues.

Second, the Reformation emphasized that salvation was by God's grace alone and no man or woman needed an intermediary in dealing with God. This was a spectacular idea that destroyed and supplanted the one-thousand-year-old practice of turning control of mind and life to Churchmen. No longer would people be held captive to the idea that they would be damned for all eternity if they didn't believe and obey Church leaders.

Third, every person was encouraged to read the Bible and make up his or her own mind as to the meanings found there. Everyone became his or her own theologian, everyone his or her own priest.

Fourth, the controversy as to the *nature of Jesus Christ* (the Christological debate) erupted again and has never been corrected. The issue of the *dual nature of Jesus the Christ* faded from the radar screen of anyone's interest. As Outler says, "the analysis of the Person of Christ came to be regarded as speculative, which is to say, useless."[172]

Since the Reformation, creeds have been dethroned by individualistic salvation-centered experiences. The litmus test for faith becomes an emotional experience. Good works takes center stage as the sign of God's presence in one's life. Thus, pietism fed an incipient narcissism that has continued to dominate the Church's life.

The Puritans

The religious tradition known as *Puritanism* has its roots in 17th Century England. American's earliest settlers, whom we almost deify, were Puritans. The term was pinned in the 1560s on those who were upset over failures to reform the Church of England. Most were Calvinists who demanded simplicity in worship, devotion to the family, hard work, self-discipline, and strict adherence to what they considered Christian morality. Barzun sees Puritanism as a form of *primitivism* tied to a quasi-scientific feeling against Romanish superstition.[173]

---

172 Outler, Op. Cit., p. 176.
173 Barzun, Op. Cit., p. 262.

Puritans fought each other as often as they did papists and others. They were the butt of jokes. Puritans, drawn from the lower classes, were chided by English upper class for their pretense at intellectualism. Barzun serves the historian well by pointing out that "Consciousness, which is SELF-CONSCIOUSNESS about morals, brings on the issue of Toleration."[174]

It is difficult to be tolerant when morality is an individualistic, religious affair. The sharper and more intense one's religious morality, the less tolerant one seems to become. The Puritan, or religious moralist (fundamentalists in 21st century America), is quick to go to war against *sinners*. Persecution becomes a justifiable crusade, and our founding Puritan fathers did a lot of that. People were ousted from communities, women were hung for being witches, and so forth.

Today's religious and political conservative fundamentalists, if you listen closely, are in a frantic crusade to cleanse the nation of evildoers. They love the phrase, "hate the sin, but love the sinner." As much as this may alleviate fundamentalist's fears of dong something evil, it accomplishes nothing. The person who is the object of this hate-love activity only feels pain, oppression, and rejection. Only the religious persecutor comes away feeling good about himself and that takes some real mental and moral gymnastics. I suspect earlier fundamentalists felt a sense of joy as they witnessed the burning of heretics. This attitude and behavior results from using the Bible legalistically. The same rationale used to crucify Jesus has been used by his followers over the centuries to abuse and destroy their neighbors. In this religiously intolerant activity the God of compassion is non-existent.

There were a few voices speaking out against intolerance and trying to stop the mayhem and killing that had gone unabated for a hundred years after Luther's death. Among those was John Locke (1632–1704), who published an article on *Toleration* in 1689. In that tract he states:

> That any man should think fit to cause another man—whose salvation he heartily desires—to expire in torments, and that even in an unconverted state, would, I confess, seem very strange to me, and I think, to any other also. But nobody, surely, will ever believe that such carriage can proceed from charity, love, or good will. If anyone maintain that men ought to be compelled by fire and sword to prefer certain doctrines, and conform to this or that exterior worship, without regard had unto their morals; if any

---

174   Barzun, Op. Cit., p. 271.

endeavor to convert those that are erroneous unto the faith, by forcing them to profess things that they do not believe and allowing them to practice things that the Gospel does not permit, it cannot be doubted indeed but such a one is desirous to have a numerous assembly joined in the same profession with himself; but that he principally intends by those means to compose a truly Christian Church, is altogether incredible.[175]

Locke may seem quaint and totally outdated in modern America. However, across America there are numerous cases where people are abused because of intolerance, especially children, women, Jews, Muslims, and all others who are culturally different. Some sects are known to follow the same biblical interpretations as used during the Middle Ages in forcing children into obedience and faith. The narrow moralisms and abusive repression of dissent that characterize the post-Reformation churches and sects have affected American churches to this day.

The Eastern Orthodox

While Rome was expanding westward through its missions and Protestantism was gradually dominating northern Europe, the Russian Orthodox Church had become master of the East. The Turks and Muslim dominance constrained Constantinople's growth.

Peter I the Great (1689-1725) brought the curtain down on Russian Orthodoxy after a fairly conservative stretch of growth. He brought the Church under state control that lasted until the Bolshevik Revolution of 1917. Church revenues flowed to the state and clergy were representatives of the state. Religious freedom as it came to be known through the Protestant Reformation in Western Europe was, with the exception of a brief window of opportunity in 1905, relatively unknown

Summarily, as Gonzalez notes, the Reformation brought an end to three great medieval institutions, or societal pillars: the Papacy, the Empire, and tradition.[176] The world as it had been known was turned topsy-turvey. One would hope that the religious emancipation wrought by the Protestant Reformation would have taught us a great deal about the compassionate and loving God

---

175 John Locke, "A Letter Concerning Toleration," in <u>Great Books of the Western Worl,</u> Robert M. Hutchins (ed), (Chicago: University of Chicago, 1952), p. 2-3.
176 Gonzalez, Justo L., Op. Cit. p. 123.

revealed in the God-Man Mystery, but, alas, I'm afraid that's not been generally true. It did, however, free us to pursue a more tolerable human existence. My next letter will sketch the effects of the *Enlightenment* on human existence and Christian thought.

ELEVENTH LETTER

Dawn Of The Modern Age[177]
18th Century

Dear Ben and Grace,

You should be aware by now that it's difficult to cut history into neat slices like acts in a play. Previous letters painted Church history to the 18th century with a fairly large brush and left out a great deal of juicy detail. In reality, every monumental historical period sends ripples, or in some cases *tidal waves*, down through future centuries. (To a significant degree each of us is always a sum total of all previous human development.)

The Protestant Reformation happens to have been a large *social tidal wave*. The freedom from the institutional and intellectual tyranny of the Roman Church (emancipation) gave Europeans a new sense of self (individualism). Swept

---

177   Private picture.

away were centuries of superstition, papal control, and rule by divine right The intellectuals were somewhat *giddy* over the increasingly popular notion that reason and logic were the real keys to creating a more perfect world. The newly formed Humanists began sowing the seeds of contemporary *modernity* during the Reformation years. The interceding period between the Reformation and *modernity* is called the *Enlightenment.*

Historical Postscripts of the Enlightenment

The Enlightenment got its name from the enormous intellectual development of the post-Reformation period. The highpoint was the 18th century. Barzun refers to the 18th Century, by the way, as the "Encyclopedic Century."[178] That's an apt idea. Our concern, however, is to understand how the Enlightenment impacted Christian thought and the future life of the Church. To do so it's necessary to put these issues in context by characterizing the socio-political trends and highlighting some of the key thinkers who gave voice to evolving thought.

It may be, as Outler suggests, that the gap between our modern age and the 18th century is as wide as that which separates "medieval Catholicism from classical Protestantism."[179] Maybe so, although that's probably not a startling idea for a 21st century American population that ridicules the importance of studying history in the first place. I can imagine most people's reaction would be, "So what?"

The Enlightenment's Roots

Enlightenment is humanity's departure from its self-imposed immaturity. This immaturity is self-imposed when its cause is not lack of intelligence but failure of courage to think without someone else's guidance. Dare to know! That is the slogan of the Enlightenment. (Kant 1783)[180]

How *enlightened* were 18th century Europeans? Relatively better than preceding generations. Had mindless religious oppression ended? Not really. The latter half of the 18th Century is often referred to as the *age of the enlightened despots.* Victor Hugo, analyzing that century from his vantage point one hundred years later, writes:

---

178 Barzun, Op. Cit., p. 359ff.
179 Outler, Op.Cit., p. 179.
180 Barzun, Op. Cit., p. 441.

And, at that period of human society, what was the people? It was ignorance. What was religion? It was intolerance. And what was justice? It was injustice. Am I going too far in my words? Judge....

At Tourlouse, October 13, 1761, there was found in a lower story of a house a young man hanged. The crowd gathered, the clergy fulminated, the magistracy investigated. It was a suicide; they made of it an assassination. In what interest? In the interest of religion. And who was accused? The father. He was a Huguenot, and he wished to hinder his son from becoming a Catholic. There was here a moral monstrosity and a material impossibility; no matter! This father had killed his son; this old man had hanged this young man. Justice travailed, and this was the result. In the month of March, 1762, a man with white hair, Jean Calas, was conducted to a public place, stripped naked, stretched on a wheel, the members bound on it, the head hanging. Three men are there upon a scaffold; a magistrate, named David, charged to superintend the punishment, a priest to hold the crucifix, and the executioner with a bar of iron in his hand. The patient, stupefied and terrible, regards not the priest, and looks at the executioner. The executioner lifts the bar of iron, and breaks one of his arms. The victim groans and swoons. The magistrate comes forward; they make the condemned inhale salts; he returns to life. Then another stroke of the bar; another groan. Calas loses consciousness; they revive him, and the executioner begins again; and, as each limb before being broken in two places receives two blows, that makes eight punishments. After the eighth the priest offers him the crucifix to kiss; Calas turns away his head, and the executioner gives him the *coup de grace;* that is to say, crushes in his chest with the thick end of the bar of iron. So died Jean Calas.

That lasted two hours. After his death the evidence of the suicide came to light. But an assassination had been committed. By whom? By the judges.[181]

This gruesome scene illustrates the continued predicament of Europeans during the Enlightenment. The answer to the previous question as to the betterment of people in the Enlightenment compared with their ancestors, I suppose Mr. Calas would aver that nothing had changed. Historians, however, are in general agreement that there was improvement. It all depends upon one's perspective, doesn't it?

---

181 "Victor Hugo on Voltaire, May 30, 1878," in <u>The Works of Voltaire,</u> Vol. I, Part I, 1901.

Nonetheless, Enlightenment thinkers believed the answer to ending injustice and cruelty lay with human reason. Reason was seen to be sufficient to banish ignorance, superstition, and tyranny from the world stage. If that could be done, then man could create that ideal life for which all had yearned over the ages. The hot bed of such forward thinking was in London and Paris. And Humanists were not anti-religious, but practicing Catholics. They were painters, writers, musicians, and scholars who believed that men were called to celebrate God's creation and to make a better world by using their minds.

Although the seeds of the *scientific worldview* were now sown, a number of events and had begun to flower in preceding centuries, it really took control and supplanted the medieval worldview in the 18th century. Coupled with the aforementioned ideas of individualism and emancipation, these unranked attributes were:

- the discoveries of other people by world explorers subverted the idea long proffered by the Church that everybody believed in Jesus Christ,
- the emergence of a scientific worldview and the associated value of *debunking* the taken-for-granted traditional myths,
- the emancipation of thought from absolute church control,
- the printing press and its associated dissemination of knowledge in the vernacular.
- the gradual movement of peasants from rural areas to new towns, seeking protection and a greater share in the growing economies,
- the increasing middle-class led by merchants, with a penchant for sharing power,
- the continued religious and state wars that exhausted all,
- the gradual demise of the despot and the emergence of less oppressive state systems, and
- the rise of industrialization throughout Europe and the invention of the factory.

If we value-weighted these events I would give the rediscovery of science and the associated scientific worldview top billing. It led to industrialization and the new factory system. Other events obviously provided a rich environment for science to develop roots. Technological changes, anywhere in the world and at any time, profoundly effects all other societal components: political, social, economic, ideational, and, of course, religious.

Industrialization, which dramatically altered work patterns and means of production, demanded a whole new set of behaviors: reason in lieu of traditional religious beliefs, natural law in lieu of magic and superstition, capitalists in lieu of princes, large population centers, and so forth. The cost of the transition was great. Industrialization and its factory system created appalling living conditions, all well documented. Dickens's (1812-70), *The Christmas Story* and *Oliver Twist* reflect these times in England. Contrary to Karl Marx, industrialization does not automatically create sordid living conditions. Man's decisions about wages and economic distribution create bad living conditions.

The *scientific method*, as you probably know, is rooted in ancient Greece, as it seems most good ideas are. Thales of Miletus (ca. 625 B.C.E.) is credited as being not only the world's first philosopher but also first to develop the scientific worldview. He viewed the universe as composed of predictable rules. He believed water to be creation's single universal principle.

As people began to tinker with things and processes and think about things differently, they came up with all sorts of new inventions and ideas about reality. As they did, the industrial process cranked up and gradually won man's mind and ended up driving all aspects of society. The rural and agricultural rhythms gave way to urban, industrial life. The new technology developed a life of its own and transformed itself into what is called the high tech or information age. Or simply, *The Modern Age*.

Unfortunately, some elements of the old medieval worldview have survived, which is a testament to the tenacity of culture. The American landscape is today marked by many who still believe in *ghosties and ghoulies and long-legged beasties and things that go bump in the night*. The news media claims there an increasing number of people believe in *witchcraft*. I've not seen any decent research to confirm that, however. But people seem to cling to the haunting fear that something, singular or plural, is out there watching us...just waiting to pounce...messing around in our private lives.

Nonetheless, all these changes were originally initiated and fueled by the Humanists. One of the key Humanists was Michel de Montaigne (1533-1593), who questioned existing knowledge. He noted the variety of cultures that comprised the world as reported by explorers and wondered aloud what kind of truth he and his people really possessed. Was it ultimate truth? Or relative truth? If it were only relative truth, then by what right do we forcibly impose it upon men against their will?

Rene Descartes

Montaigne was joined by Rene Descartes (1596-1650), who added more fuel to the pyre burning the medieval worldview. Developing the field of analytic geometry he found in the mathematical process of deductive logic an essential paradigm (model) for all scientific pursuits. In other words, he applied mathematical methods to physical problems. He was the one who urged one to think of existence as though a blank slate—"I think, therefore I am." He pointed to the relationship between spirit and matter (body-soul dualism), but was never able to adequately explain how these two relate. Prior to Descartes, theology was the sole focus of intellectual pursuit. Math and physics were mostly ignored. Descartes stood this emphasis on its head. After Descartes's theology (referred to as Cartesian rationalism) was relegated to the minor leagues, where it sits to this day. We can go to the moon and back, but we continue to cling to a very medieval theology.

Thus, in our own time, at least in the USA, so few are theologically literate that we are easy targets for scam artists like Jim Jones and shouting TV/radio evangelists with carefully woven traps to take a gullible person's money and entrap their thinking. Lack of knowledge is a rich mining lode for any scam artist. We all appreciate the fright that hits when a mechanic says that it will cost several thousand dollars to fix the car because the gadget that connects to the do-dad and drives the what'ja-ma-call-it has to be replaced. Uh-huh.

Our naiveté about theological issues is akin to our ignorance about machines. Americans are theologically illiterate. Sunday School books and other church literature generally appeal to the lowest common denominator. The learning is no different than that experienced by the poor, ignorant peasant of the Middle Ages who naively went to the local Cathedral to hear the traditional song and dance that kept him in mental and financial bondage for a thousand years.

Enlightenment Thinkers

The flood of enlightenment ideas continued into the 18th Century. Voltaire and Rousseau, among many others, were pivotal figures. You should become familiar with the literature of this period. My task is not to provide a full-blown analysis of any one of these men but to give you an idea of how the thoughts of a few key minds characterized the century.

Voltaire (1694-1778), satirist, poet, novelist, and historian, found himself in the middle of the Enlightenment. He fought tyranny and lauded religious and political toleration but had little faith in the common man to do much in the way of governing his own life. Educated sophisticates could handle governance without tyranny, however. He and his followers were rationalists and scoffed at all the fashionable philosophical systems. He argued that history was strictly the chronicle of our progressive human understanding.

Then there was Jean Jacque Rousseau (1712-1778), arguably the most famous of his age. Although agreeing with Voltaire in some things, they differed in significant others. While both were Deists and had little use for orthodox Christianity or the monarchy, Rousseau esteemed the natural state of being and emotion, which made him one of the precursors to *Romanticism*.

In his essay on "The Origin of the Inequality of Man," (1755) Rousseau argued that man had been at his highest in his early primitive communal life. The French Revolution of 1789 was fueled by his "Social Contract" (1762), which argues that sovereignty is allocated to rulers by the people. This relationship, or *social contract*, is one of trust. Sovereignty resides with the people. "Emile,"

written in 1762, is a delightful work arguing that education should flow from a child's natural predisposition. You should read it. I suspect it's the foundation of the contemporary Montessori school method.

By the way, Rousseau's writings on the value of nature led to the pattern of getting away from the city and one's work by going to the country. Our own pattern of vacationing in such natural environs as lakes, ocean, and mountains we owe to Rousseau.

Jean Jacque Rousseau

The English Enlightenment emphasis on reason instead of religion was fed by such thinkers as England's John Locke (1632-1704), Scotland's David Hume (1711-1776), Germany's Emmanuel Kant (1724-1804) and Johann Wolfgang von Goethe (1749-1832). Protestantism had taken such a hold that the Monarchical shenanigans couldn't snuff out its effect on man's emancipation and individuality. Over time the monarch was tamed and subject to the will of the people even though hereditary classes continued. The French, meanwhile, decided to serve up a revolution and wipe out the tyrants, both religious and secular.

The United States was not to forego the pleasure of experiencing the Enlightenment. Although America's early years were marked by a great deal of religious bigotry and tyranny, so many different groups migrated here that it became apparent that no one religious persuasion could dominate the landscape. All the founding fathers—Washington, Jefferson, Franklin, et. Al., were heavily influenced by the English and French thinkers. I have often read that the God spoken of in the Declaration of Independence is Rousseau and Voltaire's and not that worshipped by the medieval Church and monarchies.

John Locke

Summarily, the ideas of individual self-determination, freedom, and natural law, all of which comprise the basic fiber of Americans over the centuries came from the Enlightenment. In fact, the Enlightenment still directs our future. Rousseau's idea of self-rule, human rights, and religious tolerance are now America's own standards. Locke argued that there exists a general rights of men to property, government, and revolution. Government, which rests with the citizenry, said Locke, evolves from property rights. In addition, men have a legitimate right to overthrow illegitimate rulers. And illegitimate ruler, or any government, is one that ignores the basic rights of man to property and/or governance.

We quickly go to war to defend these basic human rights. They shifted ultimate authority from *tradition* to the *self*. In a former letter I noted how different we were from non-Westerners. I explained how a non-Western person thought of themselves as part of a group, whether tribe, clan, or lineage. They see our individualistic focus as barbaric. I must admit that as the news media brings the activities of my fellow Westerners to my living room day after day in living color that I, too, find myself thinking that we are increasingly barbaric!

It became clear to enlightenment thinkers that reason alone not only led to good ideas but to bad ones. They were committed to the *debunking motif* noted earlier and tied reason to observation and replication in an attempt to avoid arriving at erroneous ends. A *scientific worldview* was well on its way to ruling most of human thinking. As this took hold medieval religion had lost its importance in the lives of men. Secularism ascended the throne and religious ideas were attacked.

For example, On *All Saints Day*, November 1, 1755, at 9:40 A.M., an earthquake hit Lisbon, Portugal. The Tagus River flooded while fires raged throughout the city. Sixty thousand were reportedly killed. Voltaire wrote a poem that questioned how one could suggest that such an act was the result of God. The following is the second paragraph of that historic poem:

> One-hundred-thousand luckless by the earth
> Devoured b, who, bleeding, torn, and still alive,
> Buried beneath their roofs, and without help
> Their lamentable days in torment rule!
> To their expiring and half-formed cries,
> The smoking cinders of this ghoulish scene,
> Say you, 'This follows from eternal laws
> Binding the choice of God both free and good?"
> Will you, before this mass of victims, say,
> "God is revenged, their happy death repays their crimes?"
> What crime, what error did these children,
> Crushed and bloody on their mother's breast, commit?[182]

To the enlightened of the *Enlightenment* the forces of nature are not triggered or manipulated by God. Instead natural forces act independently.

Finally, it's important to mention Kant and Goethe. They were significant minds in 18th Century intellectual development and therefore to Christian thought. While agreeing on the need to jettison past oppressions, they differed on its replacement.

Kant's *Critique of Pure Reason* and his follow up *Critiques* established the idea that *objective reality* is known because the mind gives it *time and space*. By contrast, the Deists believed that God's existence could be ascertained by *reason* or feeling alone. To Kant human reason is crippled by *preconceived* interpretations of reality. In other words, we do not know things *out* there in and of themselves, only what our mind allows us to know.

---

182 Will & Ariel Durant, (eds), The Age of Voltaire, (New York: Simon & Schuster, 1965), p. 722.

Emmanuel Kant

Kant put his finger on a critical problem when it comes to arriving at the truth of anything. If you stop and think about it we culturally inherit a whole set of definitions about truth that filters everything we see, hear, feel, smell, taste, and so forth. We take in all that sensory data and immediately arrive at conclusions that are those we've already been given by those around us—family, school, and peers, who got their reality definitions from others, who got them from others, and away we go. The incoming data is placed in pre-existing structures of the human mind. For anything to be *thinkable*, therefore, it must reside in these mental molds. So, how does one break what may be, and often is, a *cycle of ignorance*? How can one know *absolute truth*?

How, indeed. That's one of the most controversial philosophical questions of all times. Science provided a means of tackling this issue. Grounded in the rationalism of these periods and, specifically people like Kant, science claims that the taken-for-granted assumptions of reality, if subjected to rigorous procedures can yield a more valid image of reality. Our knowledge does not reflect what things are, in and of themselves, but as our mind interprets them. Therefore, to hone our reality it is necessary to follow a series of rigorous tests that validate or invalidate our common assumptions. Validating that which we see, feel, or hear means others can do the same thing and find the procedures to meet the test of good science and replicate the research and find the same results.

Kant was not anti-Christian, yet in his *Critique of Pure Reason* he effectively undercut the Deists position. Kant asserted that man is endowed with a sense of moral obligations, which is felt as a categorical imperative. Those most keenly aware of this moral imperative exhibit the highest quality of humanity and are pleasing to God. And all this meant that man has the ability to understand things without the aid of some elitist authority standing over him. People can read the scriptures without being told by priest, bishop, pope—and let's add *my neighbors*—what to believe.

Summarily, future generations of theologians dealing with the issue of faith and reason had to wrestle with Kant.

Johann Wolfgang von Goethe (1749–1834), a *Romanticist* who tempered the *rational* ideals of the Enlightenment, gave the world some great literature. His emphasis on feeling drove the emerging notion of self-consciousness, or individualism. In his poem *Prometheus* Goethe insists that men believe in themselves, not in *gods*, an idea that might be the maxim for the entire *Romantic* period.

Goethe is said to have worked on his drama *Faust* his whole life, beginning in the 1770s and finishing sixty years later. As scholars have oft pointed out, *Faust* not only challenges traditional religion but also trumpets the birth of modernity and the end of medieval society. Progress is unattainable if men don't break the mental shackles of the past.

The following excerpt from *Faust* illustrates Goethe's basic perspective.

> What you don't feel, you will not grasp by art,
> Unless it wells out of your soul
> And with sheer pleasure takes control,
> Compelling every listener's heart,
> But sit—and sit, and patch and knead,
> Cook a ragout, reheat your hashes,
> Blow at the sparks and try to breed,
> A fire out of piles of ashes!
> Children and apes may think it great,
> If that should titillate your gum,
> But from the heart to heart you will never create.
> If from your heart it does not come.
>
> —*Faust I*

Summarily, *enlightened* man was optimistic that he could create an independent, happy, and productive society if free from religious yokes and despotic rulers. While few admitted to being anti-Christian, the prevailing theology was Deistic. At best, I suppose, it would be fair to say that God was reduced to being part of the natural order of things, but not an important part in most cases. Humanity was center stage.

This optimism, however, has been tempered over the last few centuries. Many people, in the depths of their hearts, no longer have the confidence that humans, in and of themselves, can create through science and technology that perfect world. Although we've made great medical advances and created enormous technical advances that have enhanced our life's comforts, we also created missiles and biological weapons enough to raise the specter of the final apocalypse. Due to science the world's population is now over six billion. Literacy is worldwide and there's an overabundance of reading material, magazines, newspapers, or books, and people around the globe are tied together on the Internet. And, alas, there's worldwide television showing us that we don't yet know how trivial and inane we humans can be.

Humankind's emphasis upon itself has led to a mixed bag of results. What it has not done is reduce the inherent predisposition to abuse, mutilate, and kill one another in the name of *right* and God.

The Church and Sects

As the Enlightenment built on the Reformation's anti-papal sentiment, summed up in Luther's idea that every man is his own priest, more churches, or sects, emerged. A gaggle of spiritualist sects emerged and were known as Pietists.

First, Jacob Boehme (1575-1624), a wandering cobbler, had numerous visions and wrote many tracts. Upon his death he had a following in England. His beliefs were a mix of magic, occultism, and alchemy.

Second, George Fox (1624-1691) founded the *Friends,* or Quaker movement. Interestingly, he was also a cobbler. Maybe there was something in cobbling that led one into spiritualist channels. The Friends have been characterized by their rejection of much Christian tradition, especially as it relates to the liturgy. And they are known for their unwavering commitment to religious tolerance and peace. Their pacifism is well known. Fox felt an inner light that he defined as the presence of God and taught that it is the only path of godly knowledge. The most famous Quaker was William Penn, who founded the state of Pennsylvania. Penn, by the way, is largely responsible for the religious tolerance aspects of the U.S. Constitution.[183]

Emanuel Swedenborg (1688-1772) is another of the key spiritualists during the 17th and 18th centuries. He was from an aristocratic family and not a cobbler. He also experienced a miraculous vision that enabled him to see eternal truths.

---

183   Gonzalez, Juston L. <u>Op. Cit., p. 203.</u>

Germany's Philipp Jakob Sener (1635-1705), a staunch Lutheran pastor, is generally regarded as the father of pietism.[184] He started numerous Bible study and devotional groups that he called "colleges of piety."[185]

The greatest organizational pietistic impact, however, was made by John and Charles Wesley. John Wesley, an Anglican minister until his death, led an evangelistic movement in England that led to the founding of the Methodist church. George Whitefield led the movement in America. These men were banned from Anglican pulpits, which drove them into street preaching, where they gathered great crowds. They became known as Methodists because the Wesley's advocated living by rules and methods. Francis Asbury and Thomas Coke established the movement in America in 1771. It has been said that the Methodists *preached, prayed, sang, hollered, groaned, rolled on the ground, and then preached some more.*

John Wesley

The Wesleys were influenced by the Moravians, a sect also known as the Brethren that had its beginning in the 15th century by the Bohemian followers of John Hus. Hus, by the way, a religious reformer and Czech national hero, was one of those unsung heroes of the Protestant Reformation. He railed against papal abuses at the Council of Constance in 1414, a century before Luther tacked his ninety-five theses to the Wittenberg Church doors. Hus, for all his antagonism to the Roman Church, was arrested and burned at the stake in 1415.

Although not as emotionally demonstrative as the Methodists, Moravians adhered to a simple worship, strict discipline, and used the Bible as a *rulebook*. Although almost exterminated during the Thirty Years War (1618-48) because of religious intolerance, they started migrating to America, along with numerous other sects, in the 18th Century.

In America sects gradually overran the staid Puritans. Many emigrated from Europe while others were *American made*. Most of the Puritan sects were characterized by emotionalism, much like the Methodists. The *Shakers*, who grew out of the English Quakers, but started here, were known to be highly emotional. While Shakers emphasized the second coming of Christ, they were highly ecstatic during meetings.

---

184 Ibid. p. 204.
185 Ibid.

In the early years Puritans made life so uncomfortable for waves of newcomers they either blended in or moved on. Richard Hooker, for example, led his followers west, over the hills, and founded Hartford (Stephen Post, our early ancestor, came to America with the Hooker group). Meanwhile, to the south, Calvinist Presbyterians, Quakers, and Mennonites, who shared similar views on life, settled the Carolinas and Middle colonies. As Catholics settled the Maryland area, they too came to share the Calvinist devout, hard-work worldview.

Interestingly, by the 1700s many of these early, pious Calvinists became infected by secularism, while others traded in their piety for a religious formalism that transformed what had been their God of grace into a tough Old Testament judge. The compassionate and loving God of the God-Man Mystery had been successfully domesticated in the New World.

It must also be acknowledged that the early American immigrant sects came primarily from the working or lower classes. These new sects represented a return to primitivism.[186] The upper classes, while amused and somewhat tolerant of all this, were more interested in the arts and the development of science. (I'll discuss the further development of the American churches in a future letter.)

Then, in America around 1740 a strange thing happened. A revival, or *Great Awakening*, took hold of the country. Throngs of people gathered to sing, pray, and hear preachers preach. The Wesleys stepped up and led this revival movement. It seemed to be triggered by people looking for an alternative to the new scientific rationalism. Not all Christians supported this reviving. Men like Charles Chauncey, pastor of First Church of Boston and a member in the *Old Lights*, a Presbyterian splinter group, and a rationalist-humanist, aggressively opposed the revival movement. But it didn't stop the movement. In addition to the Wesleys, Calvinists George Whitfield, Johnathan Edwards, and Gilbert Tennent rose to national prominence as evangelists.

Christian Thought During the Enlightenment

Whatever its effect in the secular realm, and they were considerable, the Enlightenment stuck a dagger deep into the heart of the Europe's religious soul from which Western people have never recovered. While skinning away the

---

[186] See Barzun's discussion of primitivism, Op. Cit.

historic Old World attire, the intellectuals donned a generalized notion of God, or Deism.[187] This pattern spread to the United States. Other than this generalized idea of God, nothing replaced historic Christian orthodoxy. Protestantism should have filled that vacuum but it didn't. It promised to be simpler to understand but ended up offending deists and philosophers. The deists and philosophers were convinced that the only valid way to judge truth was through *reason* and not *revelation*. *Second,* Protestantism's emphasis on *original sin* offended the Romantics and the Humanists who emphasized man's goodness, ability, and creativity. The latter believed, as I noted earlier, that man had the capability to create the good life, the Garden of Eden here on earth. *Third,* Protestantism's sense of history, warped by an otherworldly mysticism still tainted by superstition, bothered most people using reason in place of tradition. Protestantism became the *same song, second verse* of medieval abuse and oppression. Protestantism has become a weak influence in secular Europe.

These early fathers of our religious freedom on both continents would probably faint in disbelief at how easily their 21st Century heirs turned so easily to mindless patterns of conformism and authoritarianism in the face of hopelessness. The religious environment during these times has also been characterized as a feud between the *pietists* and the *rationalists*. Both were intolerant of the other side. *And so it is to this day.*

And in America we are the heirs of those early *pietists* (or spiritualists) and *rationalists* (secularists), with the former being the most intolerant. They've taught us, as Outler says, not to think, but "simply huddle around some glowing fire of the spirit and give thanks to God that it is not learning that saves a man and it is not theological dialogue that converts the soul."[188]

The French Revolution of 1789 resulted from the rationalistic flurry that jettisoned the past during these centuries. The French Revolution was a birth trauma for the West. It finalized the emergence of *modernity* and acknowledged the death of the past. The changes were so vast that we can no longer understand, much less converse, with anyone prior to the Enlightenment. For example, we who think whatever we will would certainly have a difficult time understanding a pre-Enlightened European who, when asked for an opinion, had to look for

---

187 Read, for example, John Ray's *The Wisdom of God Manifested in the Works of Creation,* John Locke's *The Reasonableness of Christianity,* and John Toland's *Christianity Not Mysterious.*
188 Outler, Op. Cit., p. 182.

an authority figure before answering. The answer would have been the accepted authoritarian premises established by the Church.

It may help you grasp the difference among these periods if I summarize their emphases:

Enlightenment (and Romanticism) emphasized *self-consciousness,* with the free expression of emotion, Classical or Orthodox Christianity's focus on God (such as it was), Renaissance turned its attention to nature and nations, and Modernity focuses on the individual.

Romanticism, that slippery and ill-defined era, is in parenthesis above because the rationalism of the Enlightenment and the sentimentality of Romanticism seem to me to be two sides of a single coin in the revolution leading to the radicalization of the Self. Romanticism and the Enlightenment are both parents of our current narcissism. They both aimed for the same goal, which was to liberate humankind from the shackles of all traditions. The Romantic tradition, by the way, is found in Rousseau, Schlegel, Goethe, Schleirmacher, Shelley, Byron, Browning, Tennyson, the New England transcendentalists, Dylan Thomas and John-Paul Sartre.[189]

It's vital that you understand that the Enlightenment turned what had been the traditional vision of Jesus Christ on its head. *Whereas the orthodox view throughout the Middle Ages had been fixated on Jesus's divinity at the exclusion of his humanity, the Enlightenment focused exclusively on Jesus' humanity.* That should come as no surprise, given the new emphasis on man and man alone.

The result of this change during the Enlightenment was to rescue Jesus Christ from all the former creeds and dogmas. This was attempted by means of historical reconstruction. That is, it led people to search for the historical Jesus. The thinking went like this: If we can discover the *real Jesus*, as opposed to those dogmatic, supernatural myths so long used to present him, then we will have something valid to believe in—an encounter with the *real Jesus of history*.

---

189 Outler, Op. Cit., p. 183.

Or, to simplify the issue, these *back to Jesus* advocates seem to say,

Let's do away with the *kerygma* (earliest evangelistic message), because it was a fabrication of those early Christians, and you know how ignorant they were. Then we need to peel away the early dogma, because that was polluted by Greek philosophical ideas, and you know what a bunch of polytheists they were. Paul got all embroiled with those Greek fellows and complicated everything. So, let's get to the real core of the faith and find the real Jesus!

This should give you a flavor of 18th Century and its legacy. My next letter will sketch the Church's evolution during the 19th and 20th centuries, with a continued emphasis on the development of Christian thought.

TWELFTH LETTER

The Fractured Church
1900–Present

> Humpty Dumpty sat on the wall.
> Humpty Dumpty had a great fall.
> All the king's horses, and all the king's men,
> Couldn't put Humpty together again.

Dear Ben and Grace,

The history of the Protestant, non-Roman, Churches since the 18th century is a mixed bag. Continual internecine warfare continues to fracture this wing of the Church's body. The Church is now many churches. And like Humpty Dumpty, "all the king's horses, and all the king's men," can't put *The Church* back together again.

New sects appear almost daily, especially in America. Suspicion, animosity, fear, and even downright hatred taint relations among the various churches: when there is any relationship. Each church is like a *tribe* with its own logo, special mission statement, unique admission litmus tests, and a litany of behaviors that indelibly mark one tribe's members as different from others. Most overt strife in religiously pluralistic American communities is avoided by a general agreement among the citizenry not to discuss religion.

Meanwhile, the historic Roman Catholic Church, with some deep wounds, continues to lumber along ensconced in its walled Roman citadel, seemingly oblivious to most changes in the world about them. Now and again, some fresh winds of modernity blow through those hallowed halls, but the ancient apparatus maintains itself. It has a life of its own. Most Catholics seem to appreciate the *changeless* character of the institution. That staid history gives them confidence, or as one active Catholic layman said to me, "It's the one dependable anchor I've got to hold onto in this turbulent world." (But things are not always what they seem. Wolfe's sociological study indicates that American Catholicism is being changed by the same cultural forces affecting Protestantism and giving rise to new forms of evangelicalism and Pentecostalism.)[190]

Meanwhile, the non-Roman churches, sects, and odd ventures parading as Christian, are anything but *staid*. Change is the order of the day for these tribal groups lest one gets left behind in the pursuit of new members. Most of these tribes have bought into what a friend of mine calls the "gimmickry of Madison Avenue" hook, line, and sinker. Toothpaste, candy bars, razor blades, and churches are hawked through the media on a daily basis. Church has become *theater* for most and beliefs are relatively unimportant for a majority of these new tribes.

Before discussing the development of Christian thought during the 19th and 20th centuries, you should be aware of some critical secular thinkers that affected Christian thought during this period.

Secular Thought That Affected the Development of Christian Thought

Sigmund Freud[191]

As you probably know, the 19th century was marked by a series of wars. In the midst of it all, however, there emerged three pivotal figures: Freud, Darwin, and Marx. They were pivotal because each forced the world to think differently about itself. Especially Christendom.

Freud, born in Moravia in 1856, was a scientist who told us more about ourselves than we wanted to know. Interested in how the mind functioned at the subconscious level, he saw man as a biological organism operating much like other animal organisms, seeking to fulfill basic survival needs, but having a more complex

---

190 Wolfe, Op. Cit., see pages 14-15, 48-49, 53, 59, 117-25, 169, 259-263.
191 Permission to use Freud's picture given by Dr. Ian Pitchford, Omaha, Nebraska.

composure. Although soul-less, man is endowed with an unconscious level that hides irrationally primitive and potentially destructive impulses. One or more of these primordial emotions breaks through to the conscious level occasionally, creating havoc for the individual and sometime society. People work at keeping these more primitive and socially destructive urges hidden in the unconscious, for they are painful to deal with when they erupt in the cold light of day.

Freud's work has had a deep impact on the Western psyche in general, and Christian thought in particular. It's been difficult for Christians to admit to having deep-seated urges for power, lust, fear, hate, and killing. While pointing out these flaws in others, we generally refuse to admit having such demons ourselves. To admit to having such is often embarrassing. We discard the memory of these childhood nightmares as innocent and meaningless nonsense. We also admit to being happy when we are able to suppress these in our later subconscious.

Freud shocked 19th century pietistic societies by obliterating the boundaries between the good and evil. The claim to be unsullied by the world, or sinless, was no longer an easy claim for Christians to make. Now secular evidence for the biblical notion of human depravity emerged.

Certainly the various Protestant churches and sects have, for the most part, not been happy with Freud's work. To many Christians, especially conservatives, Freud is seen as a psychic charlatan (assuming they read his work and understood it). Freud's notions of the *self* have had an indelible impact upon western man's self-understanding.

Charles Darwin (1809), another scientist, also taught us something about ourselves we didn't want to know. In fact, most Christian fundamentalists still live in denial of the biological evolutionary record pointed out by Darwin and further developed by paleontologists and anthropologists over the years.

After a great deal of study Darwin found himself aboard the HMS Beagle on a mission to study the wildlife of South America. His five-year stint led to the publication of *The Origin of the Specie,* in 1859. He concluded that all life evolved through various levels of complexity, from simple to complex. That included humans.

After shattering the literal interpretation of the biblical creation story, Darwin compounded his public relations image by arguing that humankind had evolved from an early primate form. Although a man's wife might call her husband a *big ape* from time to time, it's an entirely different matter when an outsider insinuates that hubby's evolution is an historical truth. Now the trouble began.

Many fundamentalist Christians take the biblical creation stories literally and cannot accept evolution as truth. There are some things that are always with us, and such literalists are one of those. There's little difference in this denial and that of the *flat-earthers*, or that the sun is the center of our universe, or the denial that U.S. astronauts went to the moon, and so forth. Darwinian evolution continues to rankle Christian fundamentalists.

Charles Darwin

The third pivotal 19th century figure was Karl Marx (1818-1833). Scholars think of Marx's intellectual output as having two periods: an *early Marx*, the sociologist, epitomized in the *Economic & Philosophical Manuscripts of 1844;* and the later Marx, represented by his post-1844 political activity and writing. His early sociological analysis was well done. His analysis of the evils of capitalism and the benefits of socialism, developed in his later years, were flawed. Socialism and its ultimate expression as communism didn't work. It was a utopian dream that didn't pan out. A personal anecdote may help explain communism's demise.

During the late 1970s I led a group of American college students to the former USSR. Several of us wandered into a department store in Baku, a city on the Caspian Sea. A dozen or so TVs were stacked in a back corner of the store. Eyeing these I mentioned softly, "Hey, look at the nice TVs." A local citizen standing nearby overheard my comment and, in good English said sarcastically, "Yeah, but we've been waiting six months for soap!" The communist system, while maintaining almost intact the old medieval peasant system, was not able to deliver the goods to the people. The communist collapse was in fact a result of their inability to modernize the economy. The USSR's collapse was never a question of *if*, but *when* it would happen.

Marx's analysis of the emerging capitalistic social forces, such as industrialization's subordination of workers, was important. He pointed out that those who owned the means of production and controlled capital took advantage of the worker's labor to amass their wealth. Workers, he insisted with good evidence, were underpaid, overworked, and maltreated. Profits were not shared equitably. Marx forced Christians to wrestle with the meaning and impact of such modern capitalistic inequities.

Many Christians became Marxist, especially in Latin America and Europe. In reality, however, Marxist systems have not worked. While trying to take care of everyone's material needs, the system smothers people's drive to produce something of value. Marxism only enriches the political elite. The moral of this, it seems to me, has to do with acknowledging that people want and need significant control over their lives. They want to create their own future. In the 20th century people throughout the world now understand the meaning of the American and European political Revolutions. This is not to say that capitalism doesn't have its problems, it certainly does (recent scandals, such as Enron, et. al., reveal some of these).

Not only did I find a peasantry in the old Soviet Union but also in the People's Republic of China during numerous trips in the 1970s and 1980s. Reports from business associates in South Korea reported the same conditions existed in North Korea (and still do). Marxist despots have never been interested in modernizing the lives of the masses. They are only interested in maintaining control for the personal benefit of themselves and their cronies. The old agrarian peasant system has been maintained as I write.

When the lid blows off a Marxist system, as it did in the USSR in the early 1990s, the peasantry is revealed to the world. Initially people freed from such repressive systems respond in stunned silence, as did the Jewish prisoners at Dachau, Auschwitz, etc., when the prison gates were thrown open and they could leave. How long does it take the average person to overcome a 30-40-50-year learning gap? How and where does one learn to manage his or her own life after a lifetime of subordination and fear? No one knows the answer. But we do know that the transition is incredibly difficult and painful.

Summarily, Freud, Darwin, and Marx sent shock waves throughout the church that are echoing to this day. Obviously there were other thinkers that made great contributions to the American culture. I would be without honor, however, if I didn't mention these three pivotal figures. Most contemporary American Christians have not read the works of these men first hand. They've heard *about them*. These three men are viewed by most Christians as *evil, evil, evil*. And it's a pretty sure bet that the pastor or lay person making snide and demeaning remarks has never read Freud, Darwin, or Marx. Which raises another question.

Why is it we think of ourselves as such educated people? I've rarely heard an intelligent discussion in the church about these three pivotal thinkers. In fact, although you will find a Christian now and then who has read a Reader's Digest article about Freud, Darwin, or Marx—which is not an acceptable means of discerning the truth about anything, by the way—you will rarely find a Christian who has read the original works of these men. Never allow such *group think* to dictate your intellectual pursuits. Read the original writings by Freud, Darwin, and Marx. Know what they said, *not what others say they said.*

Christianity and War in the USA

To say that human history during the 19th and 20th centuries is basically the story of wars is not without merit. *It may be more accurate, however, to see all of human history as an epic tale of man's inhumanity to man.* Our forefathers believed that WWI would be "the war to end all wars." Then it was WWII. And so on and on it goes. War seems to be endemic to modern man. Sometimes I think we love it too much.

Corpses in mass grave at Auschwitz

Maybe Freud was right when, in an article written in 1915, when he noted that war resulted from man's deep-seated primitive instincts. Maybe war and killing is the primitive self's attempt to throw off the burdensome yoke of civilization. We never discuss this aspect of war. Instead, we rationalize our wars to make them palatable. More important for my purpose is the fact that we always have a knack of installing the compassionate Christ as Commander-in-Chief. Well, on second thoughts he's at least our *poster boy*.

Turning specifically to the American landscape, our nation began with a war, the American Revolution. Since that time we've fought the War of 1812, Mexican War, Civil War, Spanish-American War, WW I, WW II, Korean War, Vietnam War, the Gulf War, a Bosnian war, and two wars in Iraq. And we sent forces into Grenada, Panama, and Somalia. A conservative estimate of deaths from these conflicts, exclusive of wounded and maimed, total approximately 1,570,000.[192] That's a lot of young lives snuffed out before their time.

---

192 Civil War Center.

Of these conflicts, the Civil War is probably our Nation's *defining moment*. Historians say it established the character of the American people. The wounds of that war still exist just below the surface of the national body; and that, by the way, is not to demean the importance of World Wars I and II. It is to say that the Civil War constitutes the major watershed in American life. That's the point at which we became a Nation, as opposed to an assortment of quasi-independent states. It also, in my opinion, ended America's youthful innocence. We still feel guilty that we rose up and slaughtered our neighbors, sons, fathers, brothers, cousins, and decimated our land.

In my opinion the Civil War altered our Christian thought, for as children of the *Enlightenment* and *Romanticism* we deeply believed in human goodness and our intellectual ability to create a more Christ-like society. The Civil War shattered that idea.

Both sides in the Civil War assumed the *righteousness* of their cause, which is the case in all wars. As I recall, Robert E. Lee's statement at Appomattox reflected his belief that the North's victory was God's declaration of right. (There's an old adage that many still believe: "Might makes Right.")

Religious affiliation, by the way, was not an issue in the Civil War, as Methodists fought Methodists, Congregationalist fought Congregationalist, and so on. Religious beliefs and institutional affiliations were no longer a concern, as they were in many European wars. All religious issues had been sufficiently subordinated to serve political ends.

Whereas in Europe there had been an eternal battle between the superiority of government and Church, politics and religion, those issues were laid to rest in the new America. Everything now served the state. The political domain won that battle. It was obvious to the founding fathers that religion, as it had been heretofore constituted, was a divisive force and, therefore, must be subordinated to national interests. Our founding fathers, by the way, held to a generalized belief in God. They were generally *Deists*. And there is a great deal of difference between a Deist and a Christian.

The framers and founders of the U.S. Constitution knew exactly what they were doing by omitting mention of God. They intended to create a nation whereby the state could not interfere with religious matters AND, concomitantly, religious institutions could not interfere with state matters.

Adams, Jefferson, Madison, et. al., were dedicated to the principle of Church and state separation. They were aware of the centuries of religious conflict in Europe. However, with the Protestant revival of the early 19th century, Adams wrote to Jefferson, saying:

> "Oh! Lord! Do you think that a Protestant Popedom is annihilated in America? Do you recollect, or have you ever attended to the ecclesiastical Strifes in Maryland, Pennsylvania, New York, and every part of New England? What a mercy it is that these People cannot whip and crop, and pillory or roast, *as yet* in the U.S.! If they could they would."[193]

I suspect his concern was well taken. Meanwhile, how can people of faith and human conscience not feel guilt and agony over the treatment of the American Indians by our early Anglo-European settlers? How can we not feel shame at the brutal importation of African slaves and their barbaric treatment over the years? How can we justify the Church's silence in the midst of all this and the Jewish Holocaust?

Every neighborhood, town, city, and state have inhuman acts of their own to add to a compendium of man's inhumanity to man. As I've oft stated in previous letters the litmus test for Christian behavior, consciously or unconsciously, in any age is the manifestation of love and compassion. Only love and compassion. Not belief.

It doesn't matter if one hides from the world in a monastery, carries a ten-ton cross from Austin, Texas, to Anchorage, Alaska, spends twelve hours a day in prayer, doesn't smoke, drink, cuss, gamble, wear makeup, sleep around, lie, cheat, steal, or whatever. That's bunk. None of our behavior can earn us the love of God. It's freely given.

On the other hand, all of this doesn't mean that the church is to *rubber-stamp* whatever the State decides to do. When we do that we ultimately turn the God-Man **Mystery** into another religion. The domestication process turns Jesus into a team mascot—a danger that has plagued all Christian nations, not just America. Once domesticated, Jesus can be used to justify any of our behaviors…but not those of our neighbors. Those who disagree with us become barbarian rascals! The Church, at all times and places, is supposed to be the conscience of the state. Its role is to question the state in all matters. There

---

193 Jacoby, Susan, Freethinkers, (New York: Henry Holt and Company, 2004), p. 66.

should always be a tension between Church and state because the Church calls the state to a higher order of morality. The Church says to the state, "There's always a better way."

Church Expansion, the Effect of Revolutions and the Frontier Heritage

Even though Christianity took a hammering during the late 18th and early 19th centuries, the Protestant groups expanded. The growth was due to the worldwide Diaspora of European and American settlers, driven by both secular and missionary impulses, and secondarily, to the general dominance of emotion over reason as the basis of faith.

When reason seemed questionable the Reformation themes were trotted out. In other words, Scripture is touted as the sole authority, *salvation is by faith alone*, and *everyone his or her own priest*. Added to this mix was the insistence that one *must be born again by an emotional experience with Jesus Christ*.

It's also important to remember that Protestantism established hospitals, orphanages, and other such humanitarian institutions over the past few centuries. Protestant churches also established most of our American colleges and universities. They translated faith into good works (a Calvinistic idea!). This awakening and its benefits also sprouted in the British Isles, Australia, Canada, and New Zealand.

Once the churches in America cut the umbilical cord with England, eighteen or nineteen centuries of European Church tradition began to fade from memory. It might be true to say that those centuries held unpleasant memories and were not difficult to forget. But the loss of this critical part of our Church history cost us more than we know or are willing to admit.

Revolutions are like that. Anything that reeks of the old ways is rejected out of hand. In their angry protest the Protestant Reformers jettisoned many positive aspects of the Roman Church, especially monasticism and the rich theological fabric of the early centuries. Ironically, these same Protestant Reformers strongly adhered to the traditional Church's practice of torture and killing. How smart was that? In the political area, the French Revolution did the same thing. While eradicating what they considered a tyrannical despotism, the

French turned right around and installed another tyranny. And they did all this as they spouted the ideals of equality and fraternity.

Those who laid the foundations of the post-Reformation Church were children of the Enlightenment and were either rationalists or romanticists. Like our American founding fathers, these post-Reformation churchmen were more Deist than Christian. They sought to establish St. Augustine's *City of God*, a more ideal human community based upon the positive aspects of Christianity. But it didn't work. The belief in humankind's rational ability to create a new Garden of Eden failed to calculate our sinful nature into the equation.

Relatively speaking, non-Roman churches in America still ignore most of this vast European heritage. Few, if any, know or care about the development of orthodox Christian thought and the results of the great ecumenical councils. Those issues are part of what is believed to be an *evil Roman Empire* that most want nothing to do with, *even though they are our Christian ancestors.*

The anti-Roman sentiments that characterized the post-Reformation churches became indelibly stamped on the emerging American churches.

Frontier churches sprouted and were served by theologically ignorant clergy. An emotional experience of being "born again" coupled with a *call to preach* was all one needed to become a *preacher*. The laity was convinced that God would tell them what to preach, so there was no need to get any theological training. Each *preacher* read the Bible and developed his own theology as he preached without benefit of the Church's rich theological history. Such *saddle-bag parsons* comprised the 19th century clergy crew. Unfortunately the practice of making up theology as one goes along continues to this day.

This American experience should come as no surprise since reason has always been highly suspect in religious circles. Furthermore, as children of *Romanticism*, people emphasized *emotion* over reason. Ministers who could demonstrate an emotional zeal were handed a copy of the King James Version of the Bible, patted on the back, and shoved out the back door with an admonition to go and convert the heathen. The west certainly had its share of heathen, but probably no more than any community today. On the frontier one only needed the baptism of the Holy Spirit, not a formal education to preach or teach in the church. In fact, a formal education made one suspect. This was due, once again, to the idea that reason and spirituality were enemies.

The fact that no one wanted anything to do with the historic European Churches, coupled with the denigration of reason and the geographical isolation of western communities, hastened the loss of our Christian roots. Some notable exceptions existed. Lutherans and Episcopalians seem to be more aware of their orthodox theological roots than the rest of us. Methodists have an elementary sense of their Wesleyan heritage, but not much beyond that. Presbyterians and other mainline denominations, have only a faint recollection of their heritage. The anti-papal and anti-European myths continue to stoke the flames of self-righteousness and tribal superiority for most non-Roman Catholic churches.

In addition, the Amish and Pennsylvania Dutch (two distinct groups), Hutterites, and Mennonites, all rooted in the German Protestant Reformation, are also exceptions to the general American anti-European trend. These groups have steadfastly refused to give up their *Old World* character. In fact, modern culture is viewed as evil.

The Mormons, currently a rapidly growing religious group, emerged from American soil in the early 19th century when Joseph Smith had visions of talking to an angel named Moroni in a Vermont forest. The *Book of Mormon*, by the way, is a fierce denunciation of the rich, powerful and educated and emerged along with other fundamentalist start-ups during the Great Protestant Awakening of the 19th century. The Assemblies of God, another fast growing organization, also had its start in 19th century America. The Pentecostals emerged from a split with the Methodists in the 1890s. These, and numerous others I've not taken space to chronicle, are home grown groups that shared a *common fear of the emerging scientific worldview with its secularizing and rationalizing characteristics. They were all reacting against modernity.*

A recent audit by a Roman Catholic research group listed 149 groups that fly the Christian banner. There has to be a few million more small sects out there, or so it seems. (Baptists and Congregationalists also arose from the ashes of the Protestant Reformation.)

As I noted earlier, the Reformation emphasized an individual's unique position with the God of Jesus Christ. Luther emphasized that, "Every man was his own priest." It's interesting to ask what happens when religious individualism is pushed to its logical extreme. What, for example, do you get when every person is his, or her, own priest or priestess? You get every possible theological configuration imaginable. Sometimes one can convince a few others to agree with his or her theological position and establish a church.

It doesn't take much. Unfortunately, people are pretty gullible when it comes to religious issues. Most are willing to let the other fellow do the studying and come up with the ideas. If one is *emotionally persuasive enough* he, or she, will attract adherents. Unfortunately, most people will follow anyone who believes passionately about something. People love to kick their minds into neutral and, like lap dogs, just trundle right along. Scratch the surface of any successful social movement, whether religious or secular, and you will find a charismatic personality leading a band of sheep.

In addition, once the Reformation opened up Scripture to everyone's interpretation, sharpened religious boundaries created by differing biblical interpretations emerged. Southern Baptist churches, which seem to be the most contentious group, split and splinter almost daily. The majority of times they argue over Scriptural interpretation, but it can be over anything—church buildings, election of church officers, etc. I've never understood these splits. Baptists are the quickest people to affirm that belief has nothing to do with salvation, since it is an unmerited gift of God, and the quickest to turn into creedal legalists.

Attending a Baptist College one year I remember how the young ministerial students were fractured. The post-millennialists were praying for the pre-millennialists and the pre-millennialists were praying for the post-millennialists, and both groups were praying for other groups, all of whom were praying for them and everyone else who didn't agree with them, and away it went.

The preceding reports some of the beliefs that have cropped up in the last few centuries among post-Reformation groups. The Reformers certainly didn't believe one could believe just anything, willy-nilly. While arguing that salvation was a personal thing between God and the individual, the task of creating creedal faith statements was left to the various churches. Most of the Reformers had little tolerance for those who dared to disagree with their scriptural interpretations.

The Development of Christian Thought

A new group of theologians emerged in the 19th century and tried to restate Enlightenment theology in a way they believed would make it a more intelligible Protestantism. This movement is called theological liberalism. **Albert Schweitzer's** quest for the historical Jesus is one of the main Christological strands of this liberal fabric, which I noted earlier. While freeing us from historical dogmatism, they over-emphasized the religion *of* Jesus (historicity), while ignoring the religion *about* Jesus (*kerygma*) and the connections between the two (*dogma*).[194] Space does not allow me to treat all those who contributed to Christian thought during these two centuries. The following highlights a few of the leaders.

First, **Friedrich Daniel Ernst Schleiermacher** (1768-1834) is generally considered one of the key Protestant theologians of the 19th century and the father of liberalism. He thought of faith as an awareness of the existence of One on whom all existence depends. A person of faith feels totally dependent upon this One.

Schleiermacher, like **Schweitzer** and others of this era, focused on the Jesus's humanity. Following the trend, he attempted to restate classical theology in more contemporary terms. How well he did this I'll leave to theologians to debate. For purpose of my focus on thought related to Jesus as the Christ (Christology), **Schleiermacher** picked up on St. Paul's notion of Jesus as the new Adam and referred to Jesus as the Archetypal, or *ideal* Man.

Schleiermacher argued that all other men might participate in Jesus's ideal God-consciousness over a period of time. Some theologians refer to this God-consciousness as a feeling of absolute dependence. Sin is the absence of this God-consciousness. Redemption has to do with a person's acceptance of Jesus's God-consciousness and gradually allowing that consciousness to fill one's life.

Schleiermacher's idea of gradually being filled by Jesus's God-consciousness seems akin to the old technique of doing artificial respiration. I learned this as a Boy Scout. As you straddled the victim's back and placed the palms of the hands on the upper back, you pushed down and let up to the accompaniment of the adage: "In comes the good air, out goes the bad air." Or vice versa. So, for **Schleiermacher**, "in comes God-consciousness, out goes sin" seems to portray his God-consciousness. **Schleiermacher** also wanted to jettison ancient creeds because he felt they confused people.

Nineteenth century liberalism continued to emphasize a *one-natured, human Christology*. The disadvantage of ignoring the paradoxical God-Man Mystery is the loss of Jesus's divinity: that awesome *Otherness* that's so much a part of

---

[194] See the discussion by Outler, Op. Cit., p. 232f.

the historical notion of God as the "I Am That I Am," expressed in the Moses tale. Jesus, in 19th century Liberal terms, becomes *my friend,* a *good ole boy* next door, the guy wearing a white hat that was misunderstood and executed for doing good. This resulted in a Christianity defined solely by feelings, emotions, and sentimentality. During worship, most Christians believe that Jesus is present *because the preacher's highly emotional and we all feel good and teary-eyed.*

This emphasis on Jesus's humanity, as *the exemplar par excellence,* found its way into popular culture with books (many set to cinema) like *The Robe* and *In His Steps.* It's interesting to consider that this emphasis upon Jesus's humanity reflects the individualistic focus of our times. In other words, our contemporary beliefs about *Jesus mirrors* our societal values of the time, it is not *Jesus of the New Testament kergyma.* We've essentially domesticated the God-Man MYSTERY.

Another figure of the modern era was **Rudolph Bultmann** (1884-1976, picture left). His work on demythologizing the Scriptures profoundly influenced my own development.[195] **Bultmann** didn't agree with the preceding idea of Jesus's humanity. He viewed Jesus as fully man, but one with a salvation mission. For **Bultmann** Jesus is the one in whom this salvation, redemptive act is historically played out. The redemptive act reaches into the depth of human existence. And in that Christ event, all are confronted with a question regarding the meaning of human existence. In other words, as we are encountered by the event we are forced to make a choice for *authentic* human existence or *inauthentic* human existence.

Bultmann struck a chord with all of us because, first, in our honesty we believed the biblical language needed *demythologizing* and, second, he couched his message in contemporary terms. For example, he spoke of the *authentic life,* God as the *Ground of Being,* and a person's deepest need as *Ultimate Concern.*

Outler says, "The irresistible force of **Bultmann** in the contemporary situation lies obviously in the fact that all modern Christians, in one degree or another, have demythologized the New Testament, i.e., they have distinguished between its prescientific assumptions and its religious message."[196]

---

195 See Rudoph Bultmann's 5 volume work, <u>Kerygma and Myth.</u>
196 Outler, Op.Cit., p. 204.

The danger of demythologizing, however, has to do with its limits. How does one determine what needs de-mything? Choosing is not an easy task because **Bultmann** did not give us an adequate measuring tool. **Bultmann** was convinced that he could determine the earliest layers of the Gospels, but that was never proved to anyone's satisfaction. As I noted earlier, the Jesus Seminar group in the 20th and 21st centuries has attempted to isolate the earliest layers of the Gospel, but whether that group's product will hold up in the court of human opinion will take time.

More important, I think, is **Bultmann's** emphasis on the essential presence of *The Word*, which is the key to his Christology. He believed that it is only in the *kerygma* that we are met by God's grace. When one is met by God's grace, or *The Word*, a person must decide about Jesus.

One of **Bultmann's** main altar egos was **Karl Barth** (1886-1968), another pivotal theological figure of this modern period. Both were German theologians, as were many great theologians.

Barth emphasized the awesomeness and majesty of God and did so with nary a nod of recognition toward humanity. In fact, **Barth's** theological writing has no regard for contemporary conformity. He doesn't try to demythologize anything to make it more palatable to moderns.

For **Barth**, God comes to man in God's own time and under his own conditions. God reveals himself to a person as *The Word*, through the biblical words, and through the spoken word in present time. To **Barth** Jesus is not a representative of God, but is God incarnate. Jesus was God in the flesh. While God reveals himself to man through Jesus Christ, there is still, for **Barth**, a majestic notion to God. **Barth** does not speak about Jesus in the sentimental terms that have been popularized in our time. It has been said that **Barth** re-emphasized Reformation theology and not the theological liberalism of the rest of the 19th century theologians.

Karl Barth[197]

---

[197] Read Barth's <u>Church Dogmatics</u>, <u>The Epistle to the Philippians</u>, <u>A Shorter Commentary on Romans, Against the Stream</u>, and <u>Protestant Theology in the Nineteenth Century: Its Background and History.</u>

If I understand **Barth's** position correctly, and I may not, he believed it dangerous to confuse culture and Christian faith. I suspect he would agree that to confuse culture and Christian faith would lead to a domestication of the Word, although he didn't use that language. He seems to have been aware of how easily we domesticate and use the God-Man for our own selfish aims.

Paul Tillich (1886–1965, picture below), also German, was a third pivotal theologian of the 19th and 20th centuries. Of all these seminal thinkers **Tillich** was the only one who was interested in illuminating the relationship between Faith and culture.[198]

His experience as a chaplain in the German army during WW I ruptured his faith in a number of traditional elements. First, he lost faith in traditional *churchy language*, which led him to use contemporary concepts in communicating the Gospel. Second, he lost faith in the ability of man, in and of himself, to create a godly society, a significant element in 19th century theological liberalism. He didn't, however, give up his *existentialist* view of life.[199] He couched his message in existentialist terms by talking about faith as *ultimate concern*, the human predicament of being estranged from the *Ground of Being*. He also reminds me of the existentialists when he opts to use such terms as *dread, fear, and anguish* to describe the human condition.

Tillich rejected the *historical quest for Jesus* and chose instead to focus on the *Christ of faith*. He contended that the biblical witness is not dependent upon the factual nature of events. One comes to know Jesus as Christ not by historical argument but by participation in His life.

The focus of **Tillich's** theology centers on the human condition of *self-estrangement*. He begins with humanity's *alienation* or

---

198 See Tillich's <u>Theology of Culture,</u> I suggest that you also read his <u>Systematic Theology</u> (3 volumes), <u>The Courage to Be, Dynamics of Faith, Love, Power, and Justice,</u> and <u>Morality and Beyond.</u>

199 Existentialism has to do with idea that man is responsible for creating his own life, independent of any outside sources. Existence precedes essence. Soren Kierkegaard (1813-1855), a Dane, is its most celebrated writer. Blaise Pascal, the 17th century French philosopher, seems to have been the first to denounce a philosophy that attempts to explain God and humankind. Soren Kierkegaard rejected a reasoned approach to human understanding. He stressed the ambiguity and absurdity of the human situation.

estrangement and then talks about Christ. His answer to the human predicament is found in what he calls the *New Being* in Jesus the Christ. This essential God-manhood entered human history, faced the same life conditions that all humans face and, yet, did not fall victim to estrangement from God. It seems to me that **Tillich's** Christology is basically one of Jesus as an *exemplary man*, which contrasts to the God-Man MYSTERY designed at Chalcedon in 451 C.E. Jesus as fully God is minimized in **Tillich's** assessment.

It is **Tillich's** conceptualization of the human condition that has meant so much to me and has resonated so meaningfully with many other moderns. You will find echoes of his human analysis in the writing of Albert Camu, Jean Paul Sartre, and others.

There are other theologians that could, and should, be mentioned if space permitted. I hope you will take the opportunity, for example, to read the works of brothers, **Reinhold** and **Richard Niebuhr**. There are many fine histories of Christian thought.

Summary Thoughts

As we enter the 21st century we find that the post-Reformation church continues fracturing. We're still dominated by creedal warfare and denominational, or sectarian, alienation. Like Humpty-Dumpty there seems to be no power that can put the Church back together again. While the mainline denominations are able to talk and collectively act in unison at the national level, there is little unity at the community level. The exceptions may be local community-wide prayer services at critical moments, Thanksgiving services, or other holiday events. It is rare for all Christian organizations to come together.

Unfortunately, many evangelicals and Pentecostals view the main-line denominations with the same kind of disgust they do the Roman Catholic Church. Local laity rarely share their church relationship with others for fear it will rupture their business or social relationship. I suspect that Adams was right. If some of the conservative religious sects had their way we might see sinners flogged, stretched on a rack until they recanted, or burned at the stake in the downtown squares of every American community. The only language of love I hear coming out of this sector is tinged with the self-righteousness that reminds me of the Reformation revolutionists. At best they seem to want to try setting up another *heavenly* community much like Calvin's Geneva in the early 16th century, and we know what death and misery the unfortunate citizens of that city experienced.

As to contemporary Christian thought, non-Roman theology in America is all over the board. One can find whatever he or she is shopping for. Whatever makes one's ole heart go pitter-patter. One can find a fairly orthodox view expounded at most of the main line Protestant churches. However, be ready to find a few pietists, some touchy-feely pop-psychologists, a humorous after-dinner speaker now and then (minus any meaningful theology), or a combination of any of these.

The more conservative evangelical and/or Pentecostal mega-churches continue to get bigger. First, these groups create an *entertaining* worship experience. As I said earlier, church for many is about theater. Americans nurtured by the TV-Hollywood diet love to be entertained. Maybe I should say that we *have to be*. The choirs, vocal specialists, bands, orchestras, and general stage talent are as seductive as Las Vegas showgirls. These glitzy productions create warm fuzzy-feelings for attendees. Such show biz productions play to our narcissism. Second, these groups ask nothing of one theologically. They are not pushing a creed or particular theology. They don't want to offend or scare you off. They need your money and participation in order to keep the production going. They are an American extravaganza like Barnum and Bailey circuses. And they have been successful. Generally Americans have little or no theological knowledge.

In his study, Wolfe found that evangelicals have little faith in their ability to understand Christianity.[200] He says that "evangelical believers are sometimes hard pressed to explain exactly what, doctrinally speaking, their faith is."[201] One sociologist found that to such people "feeling is believing."[202] And, "these are people who believe, often passionately, in God, even if they cannot tell others all that much about the God in which they believe."[203] Most of this tendency is, I suspect, a reflection of the anti-intellectualism of our American culture.

In the late 1990s my wife and I visited the Sadddleback Community Church in Orange County, California, with our son. The *auditorium* held approximately 3,000 people (so I was told). The 8:30 a.m. service was packed. Our early arrival time allowed us to watch the various musical groups to rehearse and talk with some of those sitting near us. One couple had recently transferred

---

200 Wolfe, Op. Cit., p. 71f.
201 Ibid.
202 Ibid.
203 Ibid., p. 72.

their loyalty from Robert Schuler's Glass Cathedral. They tired of being constantly pressed for money at the Glass Cathedral.

The Saddleback church's senior minister delivered a very brief sermonette during the entertaining session. He described what the organization offered and what it was planning. As he did so I couldn't help wondering what the couple that had transferred from Schuler's Glass Cathedral were thinking because these future plans were certainly going to cost big bucks. Will they get tired of Saddleback asking for money as well? I imagine so. But where can one run and how far?

The next letter will attempt to bring this discussion to a close by discussing the contemporary American Christian landscape in greater detail.

THIRTEENTH LETTER

THE EPILOGUE

Dear Ben and Grace:

The history of the Christian Church, including all those sects and churches hatched since the Protestant Reformation, may be seen as a mixed review. On the one hand, we certainly have not been the shining example of right and compassion that our founder wished for us to be. Too many use the Bible in a narrow, exclusive way. The Klu Klux Klaners, for example, foster hatred of other races and religions. Others  use it to justify their homophobic feelings or the continued suppression of women. We are highly adept at applying the Hebrew and Christian Scriptures to the most vicious and brutal of human acts.

On the flip side of the coin the Church has been a humanizing influence over the ages. It developed educational institutions, hospitals, charities, and exported the ideas of peace, justice, kindness, and so forth. And there seems to be a significant number of faithful who stand against the Christian fundamentalist's brutal ideas and practices of racial segregation, gender discrimination, illegitimate wars, and so forth.

I discussed the vast distinction between being a *Christian* and being *religious* in an earlier letter. Christians are those who think and act out of compassion and love, whether they are church members or not. Religious people, on the other hand, use Christian language and the institutional trappings to promote narcissistic interests, self-righteous and abusive behavior. Religious people of any generation hide their self-interests in religious terms, whether economic, political, or cultural. To religious people God, Allah, or Yahweh, is a team mascot.

True, no one lives in perfect love, compassion, and selflessness, although some, such as **Mother Teresa**, epitomize that role. You should know by now that authentic Christians:
- focus on other's needs and not themselves,
- exude a personal humility that points beyond themselves to the Ground of their Being (the God-Man M‌ystery).

Notice once again that this definition of authentic Christianity says nothing about personal morality as commonly understood by our society. Those issues are relatively unimportant. And yes, it seems logical to assume that one who is in Christ is not involved in drug smuggling, murder, theft and prostitution, since these are not *loving activities*. But at the same time one can be a paragon of social virtue and still not be an authentic Christian.

I suspect that as you talk to others during your lifetime you will find that most can point to people who embody love and compassion. People are not admired for being Christian, but for their love and compassion. You will find many people who wear the Christian label flunk the *love* and *compassion* test. Conversely, you will find people who don't wear the Christian label who pass the love and compassion test. The latter are what I earlier referred to as the *unselfconsciously Christian.*

As humans we are a mix of good and evil, regardless of wealth, education, or social status. Sometimes we obey God and reflect his love and compassion toward others and all creation. At other times, we rebel and carry out our own will. Our rebellion usually shows itself as we vent our anger, mistreat others, put people in gas chambers, and burn crosses on people's lawns. You will see this human duality played out before your eyes wherever you go. You will see kids exhibiting both characters on the playground and in the classroom. You will see adults exhibit both characters in the workplace and at home. You will often cringe in horror at man's hateful abuse of others. The media brings it to you in living color on a daily basis. Now and again you will see God's presence as people cope with human tragedy in love and compassion. Unfortunately, since the American media appeals more frequently to our lowest self, you will see more of the evil we do.

America's *churches*, 2002 C.E.

The frenzied spawning of churches triggered by the Reformation continues to accelerate in America. There's no end in sight. In addition to all the mainline churches, a new sect, or what I prefer to conceptualize as a religious *tribe*, seems to pop up like Johnson grass.

In Wichita Falls, Texas, there's the "True Gospel Powerhouse Church of God in Christ" and the "Church of the Living God Pillow Ground and Truth Church." The one that intrigues me the most is the "Blood and Fire Church" in Dallas, Texas.

As if that's not enough, there's: "Crooked Pine Cowboy Church," (Houston, Tx), "Flipper Temple AME Church," (Atlanta, GA.), "Clothing of Power Eternal Church," (Capitol Heights, Maryland), "Jesus Purchase with His Own Blood Church of God," (Arlington, Virginia), and the "Highway to Heaven Bible Way Church" (Bladensburg, Maryland). And each of these tribal enclaves beats its own *tom-tom* while extolling its privileged position in God's eternal hereafter. Each of these was founded by people who felt a call to preach and contrived their own theological format. To my knowledge none of these sects are theological heirs of Reformation or pre-Reformation theology. They're *feel-gooders* taking market advantage of our narcissistic population.

Creative, aren't we? Sociologically America's religious *tribes* reflect social classes. Upper classes prefer the *mainline tribes;* lower classes populate the conservative fundamentalist, evangelical, or Pentecostal *tribes,* while the broad middle class is spread from the *mainliners* to the more affluent *evangelical tribes.* Afro-Americans are heavily Baptist, Methodist, and assorted *evangelicals*, with an increasing growth of Pentecostalism. You would think all these religious tribes would be significantly integrated since the Civil Rights Movement of the 1960s. But they are not. At least racially different people are not prevented from worshipping together, as was the earlier custom.

The Mainliners

Mainline denominations are those tribes born of the European post-Reformation period and that evolved into large institutions, such as the Presbyterian, Episcopal,

Lutheran, Methodist, and Congregational. These big tribes can be found in most towns, although each claims dominance in particular areas of the country.

There is, by and large, a continuity of worship and training of ministers among the mainliners. For example, you can expect to find the same organizational framework and activity in mainline churches from California to Maine. Their ministers are, for the most part, educated theologically at one of the many Seminaries scattered across the landscape. The atmosphere among *mainliners* is stilted and unemotionally proper, which reflects proper social behavior among these social classes. People who get emotional and holler "Amen" or "Hallelujah" are not generally welcomed in *mainline* churches. Youth and young couples under about thirty-five are relatively few. Mainline churches are overwhelmingly comprised of the *American Association of Retired Persons* bunch—my bunch.

Where'd all the mainliner's early vitality go? It got lost in the institutional process. Sociological research shows that every organization has an evolutionary career. An organization begins as a charismatically led group, but when the charismatic leader and originator dies an agreed upon pattern of life and thought begins to develop. Gradually the organization takes on a *life of its own* that's independent of the originator or any group of persons. Participants, therefore, enter the organization and conform to its organizational *ethos*. A patterned behavior sets up and gradually becomes the dominant factor operating the group. Socializing new members into the organization's patterned expectations, which includes a certain amount of *groupthink*, becomes everyone's primary task. In the case of *mainline church* organizations, membership is drawn from middle to upper class people seeking to associate with their social peers. And it will eventually happen to all the newly emerging evangelical and Pentecostal groups.

To characterize *mainline tribes* as religious organizations is a harsh indictment, given the distinction I pose between Christianity and religion, but I believe it to be true. In a true sense, Jesus has been domesticated, tamed, and serves as a tribal socio-political mascot. In addition, members are generally *Deists*. That means they believe in the idea of God as a basic philosophical social principle. It's something they've grown up with. Very few *mainliners* can bear witness to that gut-wrenching, life-altering encounter that St. Paul and millions of others down through the ages speak about. *Mainliners* view such emotional phenomena as restricted to the lower-class evangelicals and Pentecostals.

Yet, in every *mainline* church there are signs of Christian life. You will detect *spirit-filled* people who are excited and seek to fulfill a mission of love and compassion to their community, state, nation, and world. They stand out from the crowd when they refuse to affirm narcissistic, mindless, self-serving programs and shows of self-gratification. Their *tribal* peers look upon them as *oddities*. Yet, they are generally tolerated.

Relative to Christian thought *most mainliners* parrot their *tribe's* ideas and don't study anything beyond their Sunday school booklets. I suspect that most have never heard of many of the Christian thinkers of history, much less read their work. Most Methodists can identify John and Charles Wesley as their tribe's founders but have never read John Wesley's sermons or much of his published works. And I suspect the same is true of Presbyterians and John Calvin, Lutherans and Martin Luther, and so forth. *Mainliners*, for the most part, want a succinct statement from the *tribal* chieftains (bishops, et. al.) as to what the *tribe* believes. They accept the tribal line uncritically as the price of admission. Most members view theological study as dry and boring.

On the other hand, it surprises me sometimes to find a layman or laywoman who is theologically well read. In fact, I'm stunned! I know men and women who have read as widely as their ministers; and in some notable cases, more so. In some mainline tribes, some of the lay Sunday school teachers are more theologically literate than their pastor. Unfortunately, they are the exception, not the rule.

The future of mainline tribes doesn't look very bright from where I sit at the beginning of the 21st century. They may, like the monasteries of yore, serve to warehouse traditional theology and lore. Some tribes may unite, forming a larger tribe, as each shrinks...

The Fundamentalists, Evangelicals, and Pentecostals

Meanwhile, the fundys, evangelicals, and Pentecostals, while echoing the mainliner's emphasis on organization, reflect a strong anti-papal, anti-traditional mentality. These tribes exude a sense of exclusivity and elitism. They don't like to see themselves as products of the Protestant Reformation. (A whisper: *But they are.*)

Sociologically the fundamentalist, and to a significant degree the evangelicals, are comprised of middle to lower classes where emotions are more demonstrative. I've been around fundamentalists all my life and have yet to understand how they can so quickly stir up a creedal fight. They are zealously proud of their *tribe* and adhere to the Reformation emphasis on *saved by grace through faith*. Yet they quickly fight over the interpretation of any and all scriptural texts. It boggles my mind.

The first clichéd belief tossed out is, "Oh, yes, one is saved by faith in God's grace" If you look closely at the wording or listen to a fundamentalist's sales pitch you will note there's a work you have to do to get God's grace or his salvation. You must *conger up* faith in God's grace. Until you *conger up* some faith you are doomed to an eternal life in Hell. And they've bought into Dante's notion of Hell.

Be reminded that the Hebrew Bible emphasizes that a people must *repent* and *atone* before Yahweh will *forgive* and *restore*. The Christian Bible, on the other hand, rejects this notion of God. Instead, the God revealed in Jesus Christ *forgives* and *accepts* (restores) any and all *in spite of anything*. To the latter there is nothing one can do to earn, find, or capture God's forgiveness and love. God's love is not negotiable. One can't conger up faith because it is a gift from God.

Meanwhile, the second clichéd fundamentalist belief is tied to the first. It answers the question of how one is saved? The answer is swift, "You must be born again." Besides accosting non-*tribal* people with the question, "Are you saved?" they can also ask, "Have you been born again?" If you hesitate they've *got you.*

Many people view such recruitment intrusions, especially if they're from total strangers, to be overt signs of self-righteousness or, at best, a downright lack of civility. If you say you've never been born again, you become one of the unwashed…a sinner…an anti-Christ. Either way you're in a heap-a-trouble. They'll hound you like a pack of wild hyenas attacking a crippled wildebeest. If, on the other hand, you escape by joining one of the *mainline tribes,* they'll let you know that you are still going to Hell. *Shunning or ostracization,* is a conscious strategy for some groups, while a subconscious reaction for others. You've become a traitor, an enemy.

The fundy's ideological dependence upon the idea of being saved, or born again, is directly related to the idea of an emotional shock wave as the litmus test for being a Christian. This is, it seems to me, a narcissistic emotional appeal rooted in the post-Reformation period. Evangelistic crusades, or what Southerners call revivals, have been a key religious strategy for several centuries. Even *mainline tribes* have a tradition of revivalism, although few *mainline tribes* keep up this tradition as they enter the 21st century. Certainly not in the large urban areas. Its loss is part of the institutional career. And it may be a result of a more educated membership.

Revivalism is not what it used to be in America. In rural America a church was the main hub of social life. Revivals were akin to county fairs. Everyone came, brought food, and caught up on local gossip. There was no competition from TVs, theaters, and so forth. Now there is. Social changes have brought rampant alterations to the activities of all Christian *tribes*.

Today, here and there, fundys and *evangelicals* in a community will try to get all Christian *tribes* to sponsor a well-known evangelist. Since it's akin to heresy not to participate, all local *tribes* are stampeded into participating. Are you against Jesus? Don't you and your *tribe* want to convert the sinners to Jesus? (A sinner in this context is one unrelated to any church and Roman Catholics, Jews, and Muslims.)

Mainliners end up contributing heavily. These can be pretty big productions. The music is professional, there's a lot of emotion, and the preacher shouts a lot. Everybody goes away *feeling good*. And yes, some people do go down to the front to take the preacher's hand and confess Jesus as Lord and Savior. According to common lore, t*hey are saved*. Yet studies indicate that many people habitually go down the aisle and take the preacher's hand and confess Jesus. In other words, they are saved again and again and again. They get so emotional that they feel drawn to exhibit their commitment. Revivals are huge emotional catharses.

So what's the problem? Maybe none, but I have a few *concerns*. For example, the emphasis on emotions as a means of defining the presence of The Holy Spirit (The Word) concerns me. As I noted in an earlier letter, this came center stage with the rise of narcissistic individualism a few centuries back. It revolves around a total emphasis on Jesus' humanity and a great deal of crass, medieval superstition. Emotions free of one's moral compass and sound historic theological beliefs are prone to mischief, or abuse of others.

I've witnessed similar emotional outbursts among non-Christian religionists in Central and South America and Asia. Anthropological literature is replete with the religious, but non-Christian, ecstasies of preliterate people. When people get goose-bumpy, teary-eyed, or go into a *trance* and speak in tongues during a *Christian service* we say it's the Holy Spirit. When non-Christian, pre-moderns have similar emotional experiences at their religious exercises what do we call it? Usually *ignorant superstition*. I once watched such emotions turn a peaceful Brazilian religious gathering into mayhem as Voodoo worshipers writhed and screamed in ecstasy. Muslim (*Sufis*) and Jewish (Hasidiism, Kabbalah) fundamentalisms are off the same assembly line.

Religious practices tend to be passed to succeeding generations without any thought given as to their legitimacy, or fit, in a new cultural context. As you know, *emotion* is a key ingredient in any and all religious phenomena. Emotion is the engine that drives Muslim fundamentalists to die blowing up infidels (non-Muslims). Furthermore, *emotion* fueled the European Inquisition and led to the killing of thousands in the name of Jesus during the Middle Ages. And *emotion* drove the Salem Witch Trials and the Klu Klux Klan's burning of crosses and hanging of Afro-Americans over the years; to name a few of our most infamous activities in Christ's name.

Human emotions constitute our strongest motivational drive. Our passions lead us to do all sorts of good and wonderful things. Unfortunately, our emotions also drive us to do evil things. I, too, like a spirit-filled Christian worship service. I, too, get goose bumps and teary-eyed in emotionally charged worship settings. But it's important to insure that our emotions are controlled and directed by justifiable knowledge. Too many times people's unattended emotions lead them to become cannon fodder in some egomaniac's quest for fame and wealth.

How does one know when the emotion raised in a religious exercise is due to the Spirit known as Jesus Christ or some other spirit? Was that which imbued the Jim Jones sect with such passion of Jesus Christ? Emphatically not. Was that which drove the Heaven's Gate disciples to commit group suicide in order to be picked up by aliens from another planet of Jesus Christ? Again, emphatically not. Is it true that anyone who can shout and gyrate on stage using religious jargon can fool a whole gaggle of people? Emphatically yes. Be informed and avoid the dangers.

Interestingly, you will find the same emotional strategies used with the same results in all other religions, as I noted earlier. While doing fieldwork in Guatemala I observed Maya in emotional trances as they burned copal incense to the *dios de mundos* (gods of the world) on top of mountains or in the local Catholic Cathedral. Emotional ecstasy has been common among non-Christian, preliterate peoples for thousands of years. Its appearance among post-Reformation Protestants is not, therefore, unique. Emotional experiences are not valid means of sorting *saints* from *sinners*.

We've learned enough about mob psychology over the years to warrant a healthy dose of skepticism about any emotionally charged group setting. And, unfortunately, America has her share of hucksters. I can still remember listening to religious radio broadcasts in my youth. They aired out of Del Rio and Clint, Texas. The radio stations were across the border in Mexico and the post office boxes in the U.S. in order to maintain a legal posture. Christian preachers were hawking everything from prayer cloths to autographed pictures of Jesus. Oh…and pieces of the original cross of Jesus. These hucksters made millions.

The TV has now replaced the radio as the hot media for evangelists. (Church is now Theater.) There are some stations that show nothing but evangelical programs. The Roman Catholics have a full-time TV station also, but it's pretty boring by comparison. The *evangelical* programs are huge productions, with bands, quartets, soloists, testimonials, and an animated preacher who shouts, rants, raves, cries, and…you guessed it…pleads for money. The money pitch is still what it's always been, a plea for funds to help save the heathens around the world. Many of these hucksters (I refuse to call them ministers) have palatial homes in Florida, California, and the Rockies. There're racking in millions. Maybe not as much as the Enron executives did, but plenty.

Fundamentalism, evangelicalism, and Pentecostalism are too much about *show biz!* Some promise you whatever you want—wealth, health, miracles, and so forth. They bring in snake charmers, fire-eaters, move stars and starlets, and anyone else that will draw a crowd. P.T. Barnum would be envious. They take advantage of people's fears and lack of knowledge. And, alas, ministers become cult figures. Presidents reportedly call them for advice and prayer, all the while using them as a stage prop for political ends. I'll know it's time to give up on evangelicalism when they start awarding *cupie dolls* for good attendance.

One should not be sucked into the vortex of such saccharine versions of the Faith, as seductive as they often sound. The ultimate God encounter may be deeply moving, as it was for me, but it may not be. It can happen at any time, even while hiking down a country lane on a hot summer afternoon dripping wet from sweat and mouth as dry as cotton. While it turns one's life around, its not, for most people, a gut wrenching emotional scene.

Furthermore, the heart and soul of a Christian's life is found in the midst of the world trying to mediate God's love and acceptance of us all to those who are hurting, abused, lonely, broken, and in need. In other words, a Christian's life is really not in the church but out in the world. Mother Teresa, for example, is admired for her daily service of the ill, maimed, and hurt of India and the world, and *not for building a big church organization.* She didn't line her pockets! And she is a far better model of what the Christian experience and discipleship is about than are all the TV hucksters and clergy that populate our Country. Score another for the Roman Catholics.

Ideally, a Christian *loses* himself, or herself, in caring for those who need care. To build a big church, to rake in multi-millions hawking miracles and such on the TV, to be a pope, bishop, or minister, is to speak of one's interest in his or her financial and social status. Most important is the fact that all of these accomplishments, as much as society fawns over them, are not even on the radarscope compared to the *real calling of a Christian to be obedient to God.*

Second, *anti-*worldliness is not rooted in the *kergyma,* or earliest core of the NT message. Christian fundamentalists (including Jewish and Muslim fundamentalists) feel deeply threatened by modernity and its scientific worldview. Their fear of an evil world has created a *siege mentality* that has led to an abandonment of basic, fundamental core values. Anger and hate have replaced love and compassion. The enemy is everyone outside their narrow group. Killing the evil ones who seem intent on destroying *the faith* is legitimized. In some cases members of a group strongly believe that by cleansing the world of the evildoers will lead God (or Allah) to take direct control of human life. Fundamentalist Christians see their role as facilitating the second coming of Jesus Christ. This siege mentality leads good people to do all sorts of dastardly deeds. Even flying planes into the World Trade Center.

But you should know that the Christ of the *kergyma* did not view the world outside the walls of the Temple as evil, dirty, or sinful. The early Christian Church was not a closed society. Historically, the church was never thought of as the abode of the righteous and the rest of the world the abode of the evil.

The God-Man Mystery declared God's love for all people in the world, *in spite of*. A true Christian is a vital and integral part of the world, subject to the same temptations, ills, misfortunes, and sorrows as all others. A case cannot be made for Christians being morally superior to all others, as much as many of us would like to do so. The *only* difference is that the Christian understands himself or herself as loved and accepted by God and, therefore, free to embrace all neighbors as equals and move about serving in love. That is the heart of the Good News!

By the way, one of the significant religious by-products in America of late is the proliferation of so-called *Christian businesses*. You will find people hawking their business as a Christian business. You can find Christian construction firms, car dealerships, and the list goes on. The message seems to be that other businesses are non-Christian and should not to be trusted. This is a self-righteous fundamentalist, anti-world attitude that you should avoid. Run in the opposite direction!

Yes, you will see religionists doing good things, such as collecting food for the poor at Thanksgiving, raising money for charities, and much more. Unfortunately, too much of this activity is tainted by a sense of moral condescension. There's an attitude among Americans that one is to blame for being poor and needy, even if it's subconscious. It's a holdover, I think, from the old idea that such dilemmas are God's punishments. These dirty wretches are getting what they deserve! This is God, the *great puppeteer* at work. This is medieval nonsense.

The Mormons or Church of Jesus Christ of Latter-day Saints

The Mormon Church is an interesting phenomenon and usually overlooked when discussing Christian churches in America. The movement was started by Joseph Smith in 1830 after supposedly being shown some early documents having to do with the history of early American religions by an angel named Moroni—as stated earlier. His transcription of this material (The Book of Mormon) and the Christian Bible comprise the group's holy writ and, hence, guide to life. Thank goodness no one took my great aunt Ida's visions seriously! She hated men and claimed that only women should be in the church. Men were all going to hell. What a church that would have been!

Modern, scientific research has debunked a number of ideas found in the Book of Mormon. For example, the Book of Mormon insists that Native Americans are descended from the early Hebrews who settled in America in 600 B.C.E. Not so.[204]

While being what sociologists would see as a closed-community type organization, the Mormons are known for their temperate and highly moral character. Presidents and counselors, not ministers, lead the tribe. Discipline is demanding, for emphasis is on correct behavior and not God's grace. Nonetheless, the Mormon church has become a strong and vital force in the U.S. Its members are of a high moral character. They deserve everyone's utmost respect.

Meanwhile, thousands have claimed to have visions from God over the years. One nationally prominent contemporary evangelist claimed to have had a vision of a nine hundred foot tall Jesus. Islam, for example, developed from visions Muhammad (subsequently called *The Prophet)* supposedly received from Allah (God) at Mecca in 610 C.E. The issue is not whether Joseph Smith, or any other, had a vision. Is vision the same as inspiration or intuition? Everyone who breathes has inspirations and intuitions. Some are good, some bad. Martin Luther had some *doozies.* He often envisioned the Devil trying to get him. In our own day and time there are numerous accounts of visions. Some instruct a person to kill another, to prepare to be taken away by creatures from outer space, and so forth. Jim Jones had one. All strong sect leaders claim them.

The real question is whether a vision is *of God.* Since I'm neither a vision inspector nor a moral fruit inspector, I can't say. But I tend to be leery of visions. And you should be. What makes Joseph Smith's experience so interesting is his ability to sell it to a significant number of people. My great aunt Ida was never able to do that. And I don't think the evangelist who claims to have seen a nine hundred foot Jesus convinced many people either.

---

204 Houston Chronicle, "Scientists Disputes Mormon Teaching," August 7, 2004, Collection Plate, 4F.

Don E. Post, Ph.D.

Some Final Thoughts on the Christian Faith in our Time

When choosing your church, or tribe affiliation, I suggest you do so with care. They all have their strengths and weaknesses. They are only human institutions, for goodness sake. And, regardless of my strong criticism of the groups in our time, the God of Jesus Christ is present in every nook and cranny of this world—*even in churches*. As I stated in the letter explaining the difference between being religious on the one hand, and being Christian on the other, there are Christians in every church. And, similarly, there are Christians, many unselfconsciously so, in every nook and cranny of this world. Beware of those who sort people as good vs. bad, Christian vs. sinner. Furthermore, steer clear of those who preach fear and damnation. They're religionists with little understanding of the God-man event. Maintain the following guidelines:

- The God-man event is a mystery;
- God is compassionate love that declares and reconciles you and all others to himself through the Christ event;
- Faith is a way of talking about your reconciled relationship with God;
- The Christian life means celebrating God's love and acceptance of you in spite of your blemishes and you are called to love and serve others;
- Always remember that you are *free to live your life in celebration.*

Regarding Worship

Given these guidelines, regular *worship* is essential. Not because of societal or historic religious demands, but because it *rehearses the historic salvation drama.* We are reminded once again of who we are in relationship to the *Ground of our being*. We humans have a short attention span, so regular worship keeps us in tune with the *Ground of our Being.*

Worship among Christians in the first few centuries revolved around a meal, communion, and took place on the first day of the week in recognition of Jesus' resurrection. A joyous affair it consisted of hours of reading from some of the Gospel and Pauline letters, prayer, then ended with the communion meal.[205] Only the baptized were allowed to attend, although prospective members may have been allowed to attend from time to time to hear the Scriptures read and to participate in the prayers.

---

205   Gonzalez, Justo L. Op. Cit., 92f.

Regarding Prayer

Prayer is a highly conscious way of communicating with God. You don't have to be on your knees or in a church. You can talk to God while driving down the highway, taking a shower, or any other time. You don't even have to utter words aloud. Just share your thoughts. And remember, he already knows more about you and your situation than you do. Talking to him about anything and everything on a regular basis will help *keep your head on straight.* Hopefully you are theologically aware enough by this point to know that God's not the big Bell Hop in the sky. Don't ask him to bring you a donkey, a new Mercedes or to give you the winning numbers to the big Lotto. He won't.

Regardless of the difficulty of the situation, if you live a prayerful and worshipful life you will always be aware of God's presence. That presence will not eliminate pain, destroy your enemies, or remove what seems to you to be insurmountable problems, but He will bring you peace and grace *in the midst of life's* struggles and pain.

The Life of Study

Last, study theology, don't become anyone's disciple, and maintain control over your own life. In other words, take responsibility for your own spiritual life. Don't be a groupie. Remember, you only have three basic choices in how you live:

- you can stand on the side-line and *wonder what happened,* or
- you can stand on the side-line and *watch things happen,* or
- you can get in the game and *make things happen.*

If I could look you in the eye and speak to you right now I would say that your only authentic choice is *to get in the game and make things happen*: Those of us who love you the most will not tolerate your taking any other course. But you must know that you can't *make the right things happen* in this life without a sound theological background.

On Christian Thought

Due to the continued fragmentation of the Church during the 20th century, it's impossible to succinctly set forth a coherent map of Christian thought in our day. Obviously the emphasis continues to be on Jesus' humanity, not his divinity, which continues to feed our increasingly narcissistic emphasis upon the self. We continue to ignore the awesome, over-against-us God revealed through Jesus. If we took Jesus' divinity seriously, our image of him as a sweetie-pie or good ole' boy would not survive. Our current need is to recapture the Chalcedonian formula that emphasized that Jesus was both *fully God* and *fully man.*

I hope my letters have given you a lot to think about. I wish I could promise that your theological or spiritual pilgrimage will be a snap. It won't. As you grow older and life knocks you around, as it does everyone, you will be forced to evaluate your basic ideas and core values. Your various peer groups will work hard to assimilate you into their *group think tank.*

In addition to the vicissitudes of life you will find yourself surrounded from time to time with people who want to control what you think. Most people, it seems, are very uncomfortable around independent personalities.

Make sure you read the works of the key Christian thinkers that I've laid out for you in these letters. Others will crop up as you read. Keep your feet securely grounded in this historic Christian dialogue. As I mentioned earlier, every human goes down some drain as they live and die. Everyone deals with the meaning of life and death in some fashion. Crassly, this means that we each choose the drain we will go down. *Christianity is one of the drain choices.* And, to me it is the most meaningful choice, although if I had grown up an Arab Muslim, I doubt it would be. But I didn't. So, given my historic perspective I've chosen God's revelation of Himself through Jesus Christ. This event has been defined for me by the historic Church.

If you decide that the *Jesus drain* rings true for your life, then I urge you to maintain the following core set of historic ideas:

- The Jesus God-Man Mystery is just that: a Mystery.;
- That Mystery is a faith-event, not a scientific event;
- Read the Bible as faith, not science;

- That Mysterious event was so dramatic that early disciples talked about it as God's incarnation in human flesh;
- Jesus's God is pure and unbounded love and compassion;
- This God of love and compassion declared his love and acceptance of all humankind;
- Jesus, God, and the Holy Spirit are three different *manifestations* of the one God;
- A Christian is one who has experienced the God revealed through Jesus the Christ and who manifests God's presence through loving others;
- A worshipping community of faith is a critical feature in life; and,
- Life after death is a *hope*, not a scientific fact.

Death

As stated above, life after death is a *hope, not a certainty.* You are probably familiar with books and TV shows by *Psychics* who purport to communicate with the dead, as well as reports chronicling *out of body* experiences where people are pulled into a brightly lit tunnel and hear a voice telling them they must go back. I think these are amazing! And I hope they're true, but I can't authenticate any of these stories. All I can tell you is that the early Church believed in a resurrection from the dead and a life everlasting with God. And, of course, reincarnation has its roots in Eastern religious lore, not Christianity.
Therefore, life after death is not a certainty nor a fact of Christian life. We live *in hope of eternal life.*

A close minister friend of mine summarized the Gospel's notion of life after death well, when he said,

"Look, if the God who revealed himself in Jesus Christ loves us unconditionally, then at death he'll take care of us. We put our lives in his hands when we chose this drain and he'll be faithful. Besides, at death God is going to do what God's going to do."

"God's going to do what God's going to do," sums it up well. One should not choose the Christian drain *because* of an immortality carrot. God takes care of everyone after death. Nor should one choose the Christian life as one chooses veggies in the supermarket. A*uthentic Christianity* results from a spiritual encounter with the God-Man Mystery! Don't clutter your mind with the idea that one must *find God* or be *found by God.* Remember, God is not lost and neither are you or anyone else. The compassionate and loving *God is within and around every person, at all times and in all places.* The feeling of *lostness* results from one's estrangement (alienation) from God, but not from His lack of presence.

At the moment a person willingly surrenders his or her self-dependency, then God's presence becomes transparent. At that point it's *as if* one were freed from the *static* that self-pride had accumulated and God's love and acceptance is clearly heard. This is the spiritual encounter that people have talked about for centuries.

Most people want an encounter with God. There seems to be a deep longing for overcoming one's alienation from God. This reconnection with God seems easier to come by for many. It comes to *all people* at different times and under different circumstances. Some awaken to God's unobtrusive presence and acceptance of his love quietly, others fight it all their lives, and others experience it as a jolt. John Wesley, the founder of Methodism reported his experience in his Journal accordingly:

In the evening I went very unwillingly to a society in Aldersgate Street, where one was reading Luther's preface to the Epistle to the Romans. About a quarter before nine, while he was describing the change, which God works in the heart through faith in Christ, I felt my heart strangely warmed. I felt I did trust in Christ, Christ alone, for salvation; and an assurance was given me that He had taken away my sins, even mine, and saved me from the law of sin and death.

Wesley's description of the God-encounter is very much a sign of his time. The following comprise some of the comments I've heard people in the late 20th century, speaking of the same event, say:

I can't describe it, but at that moment I knew that God really did love and accept me.

    Wow, I felt a relaxation and confidence that I had never known.

No, God didn't *zap* me like so many cases I've heard about. I've always attended church and I developed the assurance that God loved me in my childhood.

Be careful making judgments about God's activity in others. God can and will take care of others. Keep your focus on your own spirituality. All God expects of you, or anyone, is:

an awareness that He loves and accepts you *as you are* and is always present in your life; that you love, appreciate and respect *all people*, and; *that you will live life in celebration of his love and presence.*

I hope these letters have been helpful and that your life will be a celebration of God's love and acceptance. **Remember that there are no** *ghosties and ghoulies and long-legged beasties or things that go bump in the night*!

0-595-33489-X

Printed in the United States
25921LVS00004B/298-324